More Truth in a Nutshell

Small bites of Bible wisdom for daily nourishment

John Mollitt

Onwards and Upwards Publishers

3 Radfords Turf
Exeter
EX5 7DX
United Kingdom
www.onwardsandupwards.org

About the Author

John Mollitt was born in the Lune Valley, near to Lancaster. Having worked in banking and the Civil Service, he became Pastor of Ingleton Evangelical Church, North Yorkshire in 1979. He retired in 2009, moving to Burley in Wharfedale, West Yorkshire in 2018, where he is now engaged in an itinerant preaching ministry,  throughout the north of England. John is married to Pat and has three children and five grandchildren. Their third child, Aaron – a much loved adopted son – died in 2016. He enjoys watching sport, playing chess and has a nostalgic interest in steam railways.

Endorsement

"In his book 'The Craft of the Sermon' the Methodist preacher W.E. Sangster spoke of the importance of illustrations and anecdotes. He said they served as 'windows' which let light in on the truth we are presenting. In his teaching the Lord Jesus often did this.

On many occasions I have felt that some preachers have been guilty of preaching the truth without the practical application to the lives and circumstances of those to whom they minister. It hasn't always been 'grounded truth'.

John Mollitt's many years of pastoral ministry have given him the opportunity to preach and to apply the truth not only to his own congregation in Ingleton but also to a wider audience.

These anecdotes collected over a period of time are both comforting and challenging – and to Christians and non-Christians alike.

Each one is solidly based on Scripture but applied simply to everyday situations which we must all face. They will do you good."

Derek Cleave
Evangelist, Author and Chaplain

Contents

Foreword by Dr Charles Price

It has been said that all theology is, at its heart, autobiographical. Our understanding of God is fleshed out in the personal experience of our everyday lives. We may know about God theoretically, but we can only know him experientially.

John Mollitt skilfully combines the truths of Scripture with the rough and tumble of his own experience in the North West of England, first in regular employment and then for many years in church pastoral ministry. The memoir aspect of this book is warm, winsome, witty and wise, and combined with Scripture is both challenging and encouraging. The stories are often very funny (almost 'James Herriot'-ish). They disarm us and then resonate with personal life experience.

To slightly change the metaphor, these 'truths in a nutshell' are like kernels of wheat, simple and small in themselves, but if they are combined with good soil, will germinate, send down roots, spring into life and produce a harvest.

Dr Charles Price

Dr Charles Price was the Senior Pastor of The People's Church, Toronto, Canada from 2001-2016 and prior to that was the Principal of Capernwray Bible School. Charles is a radio and TV broadcaster who has ministered in over 100 countries and has been a regular speaker at Spring Harvest and the Keswick Convention.

AMBITION

What do you want to be when you grow up? Is there a child who has not been asked that question? As a five-year-old, the answer was never in doubt. Living in a station house and with the Ulster Express roaring by at 6.30 every morning, my only ambition was to be an engine driver.

Forward a few short years and alas, steam having all but been replaced by diesel, my ambition had changed. Football mad and with Preston North End my favourite team, I now wanted to be the next Tom Finney. Just one thing prevented this dream from ever being fulfilled: a distinct lack of ability. Later, as a typical teenager, my ambitions were less noble as I desired to be wealthy, popular and influential.

> *Follow my example, as I follow the example of Christ.*
>
> 1 Corinthians 11:1

> *Be imitators of God [...] and live a life of love, just as Christ loved us and gave himself up for us.*
>
> Ephesians 5:1-2

> *To this you were called, because Christ suffered for you, leaving you an example, that you should follow in his steps.*
>
> 1 Peter 2:21

It is not wrong for a Christian to have ambitions, both for himself and for his family. And yet, the believer has an overriding ambition – to be more and more like Jesus. Any earthly ambition which dims the desire 'to be conformed to the likeness of his Son' (Romans 8:29) must be abandoned. What do I want to be? I want to be more like Jesus.

BIBLE (I)

During my ministry in Ingleton, I officiated at a number of weddings, but at one I had an added responsibility. Not only had I to conduct the wedding but I was asked, by the father of the bride, to write his wedding speech. In some ways this was more demanding than taking the actual service, but eventually I put something together and later listened when the speech was given at the reception. It was a strange experience for me; whilst it was my speech, it had the mannerisms and personality of the bride's father stamped upon it.

> *For prophecy never had its origin in the will of man, but men spoke from God, as they were carried along by the Holy Spirit.*
>
> 2 Peter 1:21

The Bible was written by forty human authors, but they were not setting out their own thoughts and ideas. Rather, they spoke and wrote as they were inspired by the Spirit of God. They were real people, not robots, and stamped their own individual style and personality on their writings. The Gospel of Mark is different to the Gospel of Luke, just as the Epistles of Paul are different to the Epistles of Peter. But 'carried along by the Holy Spirit' meant that what they wrote was perfect and without error.

BIBLE (II)

It was a dark, wet November evening, but that was no excuse for failing to stop at an unmarked road junction. The resulting collision with a taxi brought considerable damage to the vehicles, but the drivers, whilst shaken, were not injured. The police were soon on the scene, and having been breathalysed, I was offered the choice of a court appearance or a Driver Alertness Course. I plumped for the second option. I suppose you could call it a 'crash course'!

Some weeks later, as I made my way up to Penrith, I felt annoyed at myself and also the authorities. Having driven for over thirty years, what could a Driver Alertness Course possibly teach me? I joined a class of a dozen other similarly disgruntled drivers.

The instructor quoted constantly from a book I had heard of but had not read for over thirty years – the *Highway Code!* Speed limits, stopping distances, traffic signs, road markings – almost everything the driver needed to know was to be found within the pages of this book. Reluctantly, I had to admit that many of the bad habits I had developed over the years stemmed from my disregard for the *Highway Code*. I trust I returned down the M6 a wiser and safer driver than the one who had travelled up a few hours earlier.

The words of the LORD are flawless, like silver refined in a furnace of clay, purified seven times.
Psalm 12:6

How can a young man keep his way pure? By living according to your word. I seek you with all my heart; do not let me stray from your commands. I have hidden your word in my heart that I might not sin against you.

Psalm 119:9-11

Your word is a lamp to my feet and a light for my path.

Psalm 119:105

"Therefore, everyone who hears these words of mine and puts them into practice is like a wise man who built his house on the rock. The rain came down, the streams rose, and the winds blew and beat against that house; yet it did not fall because it had its foundation on the rock. But everyone who hears these words of mine and does not put them into practice is like a foolish man who built his house on sand. The rain came down, the streams rose, and the winds blew and beat against that house, and it fell with a great crash."

Matthew 7:24-27

The Bible – the Word of God – is increasingly being rejected, and the result is a moral landslide, a moral 'crash' impacting on families and communities. Sadly, Christians are also adversely affected when they fail to submit to the Scriptures. Our constant need is to get back to the Bible and to ensure that our conversation and conduct is consistent with what is written there.

I passed my driving test and forgot all about the *Highway Code*, but ultimately my neglect contributed to my downfall. As a believer, I must not make that mistake with the Bible. Neglect will lead to backsliding, whilst careful study will lead to spiritual growth and blessing. Jesus said:

> *"Blessed are those who hear the word of God and obey it."*
>
> Luke 11:28

BIRTH OF JESUS (I)

In 2016, we received a rather disturbing Christmas e-mail. We thought D and M were our friends, but their greeting said 'with out love'. As 't' is next to 'r' on the keyboard, I hope I am right in assuming that the intended greeting was 'with our love'.

> *For God so loved the world that he gave his only begotten Son, that whoever believes in Him shall not perish but have eternal life.*
>
> John 3:16

That first Christmas time, God sent far more than a card or an e-mail; He sent 'his only begotten Son'. This is how much God loved this world: Jesus taking upon Himself human form at Bethlehem, in order to take upon Himself human sin at Calvary. The amazing love of God for a sinful and undeserving world.

BIRTH OF JESUS (II)

'Can we put a tent up?' was the request made by friends of our son Andrew. We readily agreed and a largish tent was erected in our back garden. Having spent the day with us, two adults and five children went out to spend the night in the tent. Before midnight, one child had opted for the warmth and comfort of a bed indoors. The others survived the night and, in the morning, feasted on a full English breakfast.

> *The Word became flesh and made his dwelling among us. We have seen his glory, the glory of the Only Begotten Son, who came from the father, full of grace and truth.*
>
> John 1:14

Jesus 'made his dwelling among us' and the phrase literally means that He 'pitched His tent amongst us'. Jesus did not come to a stately palace outside Jerusalem but rather to a stable in Bethlehem. And He did so in order that He might live, work, pray, suffer and die amongst us. Within hours of His birth, the shepherds had been to see Him. He is the approachable Jesus; the Jesus Who wants to be known. He is the 'friend of tax collectors and sinners' (Matthew 11:19). He will receive all who come to Him in repentance and faith.

BIRTH OF JESUS (III)

When I started my education in the 1950s, the school was full of Johns, Michaels, Peters, Davids – not the rather 'weird and wonderful' names which are sometimes inflicted on children today. There was, however, one boy with a somewhat distinctive name because he was called Chester. Apparently, he had been given this name because his parents had met in Chester. He must have been thankful that his parents had not met in Giggleswick or Ashby-de-la-Zouch.

Our adopted son, Aaron, came to us already named, but when my wife asked his natural mother why she had chosen that name, Pat was in for a surprise. In the hospital, the mother had been given a book of baby names and 'Aaron' was the first name in the book!

> *"She will give birth to a son, and you are to give him the name Jesus, because he will save his people from their sins."*
>
> Matthew 1:21

> *"The virgin will be with child and will give birth to a son, and they will call him Immanuel"* *(which means "God with us").*
>
> Matthew 1:23

Today, much thought or little thought might be given to naming children, but that was not the case in Bible times. Names were given because they had meaning, and the names 'Immanuel' and 'Jesus' describe who He is and what He came to do. He is 'God with us' and His great mission is 'to save his people from their sins'.

Jesus was a man, a teacher, an example, but there have been many teachers and examples. Jesus is quite unique because He is a unique Person Who came for a unique purpose. He is the Incarnate God Who died to accomplish our salvation. Therefore, He alone is worthy of our trust and of our worship.

BIRTH OF JESUS (IV)

One Christmas, one of our grandchildren wrote to Father Christmas: 'Dear Father Christmas. I hope I have been good enough to my brother this year.' Not really a strange introduction to her letter because, when the siblings had been squabbling, her mother had said, 'Don't forget – if you are naughty, Father Christmas will not come.'

A few days later, I was asked to be Father Christmas at a pre-school children's party. Donning the outfit and ringing a bell, I made my entrance and was faced by young children whose faces were a mixture of excitement and trepidation. 'Because you have all been good children,' said the leader, 'Father Christmas has come to your party.' They all looked angelic – I know appearances can be deceptive – and so there was a present for every girl and boy.

> *"I have not come to call the righteous but sinners."*
>
> Matthew 9:13

> *...all have sinned and fall short of the glory of God.*
>
> Romans 3:23

> *Christ Jesus came into the world to save sinners.*
> 1 Timothy 1:15

Father Christmas comes for good boys and girls, but Jesus Christ came for bad boys and girls, for bad men and women. He 'came [...] to save sinners', and therefore, we are all qualified to be saved. The sad thing is that some disqualify themselves because they will not admit they are sinners. For such people Jesus can do nothing, but for all who will confess their sin and trust in Christ, there is the promise of salvation.

CHARACTER

As a village pastor, I was frequently asked to provide a character reference. More often than not, knowing the integrity of the person, this was something I was more than happy to do. Only on rare occasions did it prove to be a challenge.

A homeless young man whom I scarcely knew, after he had been evicted from his council flat for damaging the property, gave my name as a reference to a housing association. My sympathy for the 'sofa surfing' young man had to be balanced against my responsibility to the housing association. I can only hope that what I wrote was fair to both parties.

> ...the administrators and the satraps tried to find grounds for charges against Daniel in his conduct of government affairs, but they were unable to do so. They could find no corruption in him, because he was trustworthy and neither corrupt nor negligent.
>
> Daniel 6:4

> Both of them [Zacharias and Elizabeth] were upright in the sight of God, observing all the Lord's commandments and regulations blamelessly.
>
> Luke 1:6

He [Barnabas] was a good man, full of the Holy Spirit and faith.

Acts 11:24

Demetrius is well spoken of by everyone—and even by the truth itself. We also speak well of him, and you know that our testimony is true.

3 John 12

And a voice from heaven said, "This is my Son, whom I love; with Him I am well pleased."

Matthew 3:17

"Well done, good and faithful servant!"

Matthew 25:21

Daniel, Zacharias, Elizabeth, Barnabas, Demetrius and many others in the Bible, though they were not flawless, had excellent references. But only Jesus had the perfect reference because His reference was from God. And ultimately, that is what really matters. To have a good testimony before men is important, but at the end of our days, to be approved by God is even more important. 'Well done, good and faithful servant!' is the reference we should all desire.

Christian Life (I)

Whilst we were putting our shopping into the car at the supermarket, a vehicle drew up beside us and an elderly lady got out. What attracted our attention was the colour of the car: lime green but so bright we felt we needed sunglasses.

Pat commented on the colour and the lady had an interesting response. 'I got tired of parking my car in supermarket car parks and then not being able to find it, so I thought I would buy a car I could not avoid seeing.' I would consider it 'mission accomplished'.

> *The LORD was with Joseph and he prospered, and he lived in the house of his Egyptian master [...] his master saw that the LORD was with him.*
>
> Genesis 39:2-3

> *And all who were sitting in the Sanhedrin looked intently at Stephen, and they saw that his face was like the face of an angel.*
>
> Acts 6:15

> *"You are the light of the world."*
>
> Matthew 5:14

> *"Let your light shine before men, that they may see your good deeds and praise your father in heaven."*
>
> Matthew 5:16

...that you may become blameless and pure, children of God without fault in a crooked and depraved generation, in which you shine like stars in the universe.

Philippians 2:15

As believers, do we stand out from those who have no Christian profession? Stand out, not because we are awkward and difficult but rather because something of Christ is to be seen in us? Joseph shone in the house of Potiphar, Daniel in the court of King Nebuchadnezzar, Stephen before the Jewish Sanhedrin. They were dark places but they stood out as men of true faith. That is still the challenge and calling that comes to believers today.

One of the very first songs I sang in Sunday School might sound simplistic to some but it is true whatever our age.

Jesus bids us shine with a pure clear light
Like a little candle burning in the night
In this world of darkness, so we must shine
You in your small corner and I in mine.

Susan B. Warner (1819-1885)

CHRISTIAN LIFE (II)

Having stayed overnight in London, we had a taxi booked for half past nine to get us to the railway station. Waking early, we went across the road to a café advertising 'Croissants and Coffee'. This light breakfast was most enjoyable and afterwards we went for a short walk before collecting our luggage and waiting for the taxi.

As we waited, I asked Pat, 'Did you pay for the croissants and coffee?'

'No,' she responded, 'did you?'

To our consternation, we realised we had walked out of the café without paying. Pat rushed back whilst I guarded the suitcases.

The proprietor was quite unaware we had not paid, thinking that one of his assistants had taken the money. He was astounded that Pat had returned to pay, and he could not recall this ever having happened before. Pat returned just in time for the taxi, and we both began the journey home with an easier conscience.

> Give everyone what you owe [...] Let no debt remain outstanding.
>
> Romans 13:7-8

> ...we are taking pains to do what is right, not only in the eyes of the Lord but also in the eyes of men.
>
> 2 Corinthians 8:21

In all their dealings, believers should be scrupulously honest and beyond reproach. This is one of the ways in which we can be different and distinctive from many in our society today.

CHRISTIAN LIFE (III)

Having moved into our new home, we decided that the old boiler needed replacing and we engaged the services of a heating engineer. It was a cold, frosty December morning when the man arrived and started work in the garage. Pat sympathised that he was having to do the work in such freezing conditions, but his response was down-to-earth and realistic: 'You cannot be a heating engineer without having to work in cold and damp conditions.'

> *We must go through many hardships to enter the kingdom of God.*
>
> Acts 14:22

> *In fact, everyone who wants to live a godly life in Christ Jesus will be persecuted.*
>
> 2 Timothy 3:12

> *Do not be surprised at the painful trial you are suffering, as though something strange were happening to you.*
>
> 1 Peter 4:12

> *We know that we are children of God, and that the whole world is under the control of the evil one.*
>
> 1 John 5:19

The heating engineer knows the environment in which he has to work and so is not surprised by cold and damp conditions. As believers we have to live in a world 'under the control of the evil one', a world which is hostile to the things of God. We should therefore not be surprised by the hardships, the painful trials and the opposition that so often we have to face. It is all part of our calling and a sign that we are indeed true believers.

CHURCH (I)

The old Employment Exchanges were depressing places, often scruffy and poorly decorated. This was certainly true of the premises I worked at in Morecambe during the early 1970s. However, in the mid-1970s, the government had a change of strategy. Employment Exchanges had been responsible both for finding the unemployed work but also the paying of unemployment benefit. It was now decided to separate the two functions.

Consequently, Jobcentres came into being, and what a contrast they were to the old Employment Exchanges. In Morecambe, we went into a new building with carpets and modern furniture – quite unrecognisable from the 'wooden hut' in which I had worked for the previous four years. It was a building that appealed to both staff and public.

Unfortunately, the Jobcentre opened in Morecambe at a time of high unemployment and also at the end of the summer season. This meant that though we had an impressive building, embarrassingly we had very few jobs to offer. I remember the manager saying, 'It is like opening a new bakery when there is a shortage of bread.' It was for this reason that some Jobcentres became known as 'joke-centres' – because jobs were almost non-existent.

I am compelled to preach. Woe to me if I do not preach the gospel!

1 Corinthians 9:16

As we have already said, so now I say again: if anybody is preaching to you a gospel other than what you accepted, let him be eternally condemned.

Galatians 1:9

...the church of the living God, the pillar and foundation of the truth.

1 Timothy 3:15

A church without the gospel is like a bakery without bread, a Jobcentre without jobs. It serves no real purpose and deserves to be shut down. And whilst it is always sad when a church closes, it is just as sad when a church stays open but does not preach the gospel. How we need gospel churches, Bible-believing churches – churches which are the 'the pillar and foundation of the truth'.

CHURCH (II)

Some years ago, as I came out of a car park in Oswestry, ahead of me there was a large church building. A banner was on display outside the building, and from a distance I thought it said 'Sunday Message'. However, on getting closer, I discovered the words were not 'Sunday Message' but rather 'Sunday Massage'. Far from being a place of worship, the redundant church was now a health and fitness centre.

> *I will build My church, and the gates of Hades will not overcome it.*
> Matthew 16:18

> *If you do not repent, I will come to you and remove your lampstand from its place.*
> Revelation 2:5

> *...a great multitude that no one could count.*
> Revelation 7:9

Churches will close, 'lampstands' can be removed; the visible church can become weaker and weaker. But the true church, the invisible church, made up of all who have repented and trusted Christ as Saviour – that church can never become weaker. Every second it gets stronger, as believers are added by death to the church in heaven and sinners are added by conversion to the church on earth. It is the one true church with two different branches. Yes, Christ will build His church and it will ultimately be made up of 'a great multitude that no one could count'. Praise God!

CONVERSION

I was born in Lancashire, as were my children, but in 1979, we moved across the border into Yorkshire. A year or two later, the Roses match between these two counties was being played at Headingley. The match was being televised and as I walked into the room, Andrew said, 'Dad, we've got them all out.' I presumed he meant Yorkshire, the white rose county, but to my amazement, it was Lancashire who had just been bowled out. It was then that the truth slowly dawned on me that Andrew had changed allegiance and now Yorkshire, not Lancashire, was the county he supported.

> *...by nature, objects of wrath.*
>
> Ephesians 2:3

> *...to all who received him, to those who believed in his name, he gave the right to become children of God.*
>
> John 1:12

> *...he has rescued us from the dominion of darkness and brought us into the kingdom of the Son he loves.*
>
> Colossians 1:13

It is an unpopular but a biblical truth that, by nature, we are all 'objects of wrath'. Jesus told the Jews, '...you belong to your father the devil' (John 8:44), and the truth was so unpalatable to them they 'picked up stones to stone him' (John 8:59). Unpopular, unpalatable then; unpopular, unpalatable now – but nevertheless true. Because of Adam, we all come into this world with our backs to God and on the side of Satan. That is why we all need to be converted – to change sides.

The change comes when, realising our true condition, we repent and trust Jesus Christ as our Saviour. In that moment, we change sides, and from being the children of Satan, we become the children of God. We then have the desire to please God and not Satan.

DEATH OF JESUS (I)

In February 1970, a murder took place in Overton, five miles from the seaside town of Morecambe. The victim was an antiques dealer and though he was not known to me, he was a customer of the bank where I was employed. And it was this connection which was to draw me into the murder investigation.

A young colleague at the bank lived in Overton, and as part of their enquiries, the police interviewed every resident of the village. The murder had taken place on a Tuesday evening, and the young man was asked to account for his whereabouts on that particular night. That evening, as part of his banking studies, he should have been at the College of Further Education but, unknown to his parents, instead of going to college, he had gone to the cinema. Interviewed in the presence of his parents, he foolishly told the police that he had been at college. When checks were made at the college, his deceit was soon uncovered and the young man became a prime suspect.

On that Tuesday evening, I had been at the Odeon Cinema in Morecambe with a girlfriend, and I had spoken to my work colleague. When re-interviewed by the police, he told the truth and gave my name as someone who could verify his alibi. I then had a visit from the Lancashire Constabulary and it was a very uneasy interview.

As bank employees, we had access to the financial accounts of the deceased, and therefore a motive for the murder. Having been interviewed, I was asked to give a written statement, and my girlfriend was subjected to a similar procedure. To be suspected of murder when innocent was an unnerving experience and even more so for the young man from Overton. One morning, he arrived at work in an ill-fitting suit as his own clothes had all been taken away for forensic examination. Eventually the police were satisfied that neither of us had any involvement in the crime.

A local man was arrested and sentenced for the crime, but it was a miscarriage of justice, and after four years in prison, he was released. I cannot begin to imagine what agonies he must have gone through: arrested, tried, found guilty and sentenced, when all the time he was an innocent man.

Later, this man was converted and having been forgiven by God, he was able to forgive those who had falsely accused him. For a number of years, I worshipped at the same church as his sister, and having become a pastor, he poignantly told of his experience in the bestselling book *Killing Time.*

> *Pilate called together the chief priests, the rulers and the people, and said to them, [...] "I have examined him in your presence and have found no basis for your charges against him. [...] Therefore, I will punish him and then release him." With one voice they cried out, "Away with this man! Release Barabbas to us!" [...] So Pilate decided to grant their demand. He released the man who had been thrown into prison for*

insurrection and murder, the one they asked for,
and surrendered Jesus to their will.

Luke 23:13-14,16,18,24-25

"This man was handed over to you by God's set
purpose and foreknowledge; and you, with the
help of wicked men, put him to death by nailing
him to the cross."

Acts 2:23

In 1970, the police, judge and jury considered the man to be guilty, but Pilate and the Jewish authorities knew that Jesus was not guilty and they still sentenced Him to be crucified. This was just part of the suffering that Jesus endured, and yet it was all within the plan and 'set purpose' of God.

Christ died for sins once for all, the righteous for
the unrighteous, to bring you to God.

1 Peter 3:18.

The innocent One had to take my guilt, so that I – the guilty one – might be counted innocent in the sight of God.

Death of Jesus (II)

One Saturday morning I was in Liverpool, as later in the day I was speaking at a Bible convention in the area. In order to relax, I went with Aaron to watch Everton Football Club U18s. Amongst the spectators, I recognised the ex-Liverpool Football Club player David Fairclough. David was known as 'Super Sub' as he was renowned for coming off the substitute bench and making an immediate impact. He kindly agreed to have a photograph taken with Aaron.

> *...the chief priests and the elders persuaded the crowd to ask for Barabbas and to have Jesus executed.*
>
> Matthew 27:20

> *But he was pierced for our transgressions, he was crushed for our iniquities; the punishment that brought us peace was on him, and by his wounds we are healed.*
>
> Isaiah 53:5

> *"He himself bore our sins" in his own body on the tree.*
>
> 1 Peter 2:24

The middle tree should have been occupied by Barabbas, but it was on that tree Jesus was crucified. He became the substitute for Barabbas but more than just Barabbas.

Taking our sin, our guilt, our punishment, Jesus became the substitute for all who repent and trust in Him.

> *Bearing shame and scoffing rude,*
> *In my place condemned He stood;*
> *Sealed my pardon with His blood;*
> *Hallelujah! What a Saviour!*
>
> Philip Paul Bliss (1838-1876)

DEATH OF JESUS (III)

The family were coming to stay for a few days at Christmas and so off we went on a twenty-mile journey to a supermarket in Carnforth. The supermarket was heaving with people, but eventually, with a trolley full of 'goodies', off we went to queue at the checkout. There I helped to pack the food into carrier bags and Pat prepared to settle the bill. Oh dear – a frantic search in her bag and purse, but no bank card. She looked to me but I had neither card nor money.

All we could now do was take the shopping out of the trolley whilst a member of staff was summoned to return the goods to the shelves. How embarrassing and how disappointing. Yorkshire puddings, meat, ice cream, biscuits, chocolates, drinks – a plethora of good things but no one to pay for them. No card. No money. No receipt.

> *"Two men owed money to a certain money-lender. One owed him five hundred denarii, and the other fifty. Neither of them had the money to pay him back, so he cancelled the debts of both."*
> Luke 7:41-42

> *...you were bought at a price.*
> 1 Corinthians 6:20

> *...it was not with perishable things such as silver or gold that you were redeemed from the empty*

way of life [...] but with the precious blood of
Christ.

1 Peter 1:18-19

Forgiveness of sin, peace with God, an eternal home in heaven – these all had to be paid for. As sinful people, we had nothing to offer; the debt was far too great ever to be paid for by us. We needed Someone to pay the price on our behalf. And that is why Jesus came – to redeem us, to pay the price of our salvation. He went to the cross of Calvary and He paid the price 'not with perishable things such as silver or gold' but with His own 'precious blood'.

He died that we might be forgiven
He died to make us good,
That we might go at last to heaven,
Saved by His precious blood.
There was no other good enough
To pay the price of sin;
He only could unlock the gate,
Of heaven and let us in.

Cecil Frances Alexander (1818-1895)

DEATH OF JESUS (IV)

In a BBC poll of 2002, Winston Churchill was voted the greatest Briton who ever lived. Perhaps not too surprising, as twice Winston Churchill was Prime Minister, and as an inspirational statesman, he led Britain to victory in the Second World War. He was also a renowned writer, orator and artist.

And yet, for a strange reason, it is not so much the life of Winston Churchill I remember but rather his death. As a family, we never had a television, but that changed when a set was installed on 23 January 1965 and we looked forward to a weekend of uninterrupted viewing. But the next day, Winston Churchill died and the scheduled programmes were all cancelled.

They were replaced by sombre music and the notification of a special programme. 'With the news of Winston Churchill's death bringing the nation to a standstill, BBC Television presents an obituary to a beloved man and a much-respected statesman.' Not quite the weekend we had been expecting.

...he took Peter, John and James with him and went up onto a mountain to pray. As he was praying, the appearance of his face changed, and his clothes became as bright as a flash of lightning. Two men, Moses and Elijah, appeared in glorious splendour, talking with Jesus. They

spoke about his departure which he was about to bring to fulfilment at Jerusalem.

Luke 9:28-31

For whenever you eat this bread and drink this cup, you proclaim the Lord's death until he comes.

1 Corinthians 11:26

...reconciled to him [God] through the death of his Son.

Romans 5:10

I resolved to know nothing while I was with you except Jesus Christ and him crucified.

1 Corinthians 2:2

Most people rightly remember the life rather than the death of Winston Churchill, but as Christians, we are told to remember the death rather than the life of Jesus. This is not in any way to devalue His life, His teaching or His example, but to emphasise the supreme importance of His death. For it is through the death of Christ that our sins are forgiven and we are reconciled to God.

DEITY OF CHRIST

Suits were once the order of the day for bankers, solicitors, doctors, accountants, etc. but for some professions, more casual dress now appears to be acceptable. This can especially be so when the weather is hot and sultry. My sister-in-law was a doctor's receptionist, and one summer's day, a young doctor went on a house visit, dressed in a T-shirt, Bermuda shorts and sunglasses. When the elderly patient opened the door, she showed him under the stairs – she thought he had come to read the gas meter. However, although his appearance suggested otherwise, he was still the doctor.

> *Christ Jesus, Who, being in very nature God did not consider equality with God something to be grasped, but made himself nothing, taking the very nature of a servant, being made in human likeness.*
>
> Philippians 2:5-7

> *He came to that which was his own, but his own did not receive him.*
>
> John 1:11

> *When Jesus came to the region of Caesarea Philippi, he asked his disciples, "Who do people say the Son of Man is?" They replied, "Some say John the Baptist; others say Elijah; and still others, Jeremiah or one of the prophets." "But*

*what about you?" he asked. "Who do you say I
am?" Simon Peter answered, "You are the
Christ, the Son of the living God."*

Matthew 16:13-16

God in a manger? God hungry, thirsty, tired and
weeping? God becoming a servant? Perhaps not surprising
that many only saw Jesus as a man. But this is the mystery
and the miracle of the Incarnation: Jesus was truly a man
but He never ceased to be God. That is why at
Christmastime He demands our worship, not our
sentimental affection.

*Our God contracted to a span.
Incomprehensibly made man.*

Charles Wesley

DISCERNMENT (I)

Mrs E. was elderly and rather forgetful but in her home she always had an array of lovely flowers. One day, she sheepishly told me that she had an embarrassing confession to make. She had been watering some flowers, only to later discover they were not real but artificial. An understandable mistake, as increasingly artificial flowers can look like the real thing – but they do not need water.

> *"...his enemy came and sowed weeds among the wheat."*
>
> Matthew 13:25

> *...do not believe every spirit, but test the spirits to see whether they are from God, because many false prophets have gone out into the world.*
>
> 1 John 4:1

Cults and sects can be both subtle and convincing – that is why many are seduced by them. What they are saying is so near the truth, it is mistaken for the truth. False teachers, like artificial flowers, are not real – they propagate 'fake' news, not the good news of the gospel.

> *Discernment is not simply telling the difference between what is right and what is wrong; rather it is the difference between right and almost right.*
>
> C.H. Spurgeon

DISCERNMENT (II)

Three or four times every year, we went with Aaron to the children's hospice. The respite break was always most welcome and one of the attractions was the sumptuous food provided. We never returned home without having added on a few pounds. One lunchtime we were tucking into our apple pie and custard when there was an anguished cry from the kitchen. 'Stop – that isn't custard, it is cheese sauce!'

Strange, but apparently no one had noticed. The cheese sauce had the colour and the texture of custard, and the taste, though different, had not been sufficient for anyone to complain. Without the cry from the kitchen, I would have continued eating the apple crumble, but now it wasn't quite as appetising.

> *"Watch out for false prophets. They come to you in sheep's clothing, but inwardly they are ferocious wolves."*
>
> Matthew 7:15

> *...there were also false prophets among the people, just as there will be false teachers among you. They will secretly introduce destructive heresies.*
>
> 2 Peter 2:1

...the Bereans [...] examined the Scriptures every day to see if what Paul said was true.

Acts 17:11

The false teacher may be a 'nice' man, he may have a Bible in his hand, but he can still be the bearer of 'destructive heresies'. What he says must be tested by the Scriptures, and if it is contrary to what is written in the Word of God, then both the man and his message must be rejected.

DISCIPLINE

In my form at secondary school, there was an Olympic contestant. Mary was the youngest athlete to compete in the 1964 Tokyo Summer Olympics, reaching the semi-final of the 800 metres. I remember seeing Mary in the annual sports day at school and, not surprisingly, she lapped many of the other competitors.

We saw a superb athlete but what we did not see was all the 'blood, sweat and tears' that went into making her the athlete she was. No doubt she had an innate ability, but that had to be complemented by many hours of early-morning and late-night training in all kinds of weather.

> Therefore, I do not run like a man running aimlessly; I do not fight like a man beating the air. No, I beat my body and make it my slave so that after I have preached to others, I myself will not be disqualified for the prize.
> 1 Corinthians 9:26-27

There are no shortcuts to becoming a sanctified, godly Christian. It never just happens but requires self-denial and self-sacrifice. It takes the discipline of regular church attendance, daily prayer and Bible study. Am I prepared to pay the price in order to obtain the prize?

ENCOURAGEMENT

I was a nervous young man when I took my first faltering steps as a preacher. To be faced with a 'sea of faces' was not something I had ever previously experienced. However, there was one country chapel where I immediately felt at ease. Towards the front there sat a man with a shining, beaming face, and throughout the service, he would nod approvingly. What an encouragement to a novice preacher.

'Uncle John' did preach but rather than preach himself, he felt his calling was to encourage and reassure other preachers. This was a ministry he faithfully fulfilled until he was called home in his nineties. Many a preacher can testify how much they were helped by this man.

> *Jeremiah said, "I do not know how to speak, I am only a child." But the LORD said to me, "Do not say, 'I am only a child.' You must go to everyone I send you to and say whatever I command you. Do not be afraid of them, for I am with you and will rescue you," declares the LORD.*
>
> Jeremiah 1:6-8

> *Barnabas (which means "Son of Encouragement").*
>
> Acts 4:36

...encourage one another and build each other up.

Let us encourage one another – and all the more as you see the Day approaching.

Hebrews 10:25

As preachers, we hope to encourage the congregation, but the congregation can also encourage the preacher. A smile, a nod, a heartfelt 'amen' can make all the difference to a preacher who is tired and struggling. 'Uncle John' was a 'Barnabas', and I thank God for every man and woman who is an encourager in the church today, those who seek not only to encourage the preacher but every believer.

ETERNITY

My grandfather spent his life as a signalman, and this meant he was meticulous when it came to telling the time. 'What time is it, Grandad?' 'It is eight and a half minutes past ten,' would be the precise reply. 'That is the six-twenty from Lancaster – he's three minutes late.' Time was important to Grandad, and not for him a wristwatch but the pocket watch and chain which was favoured by most men of his generation.

At the age of eighty-eight, Grandad was taken into hospital, and a few days before he died, he handed his faithful pocket watch to his son. 'Take this,' he said. 'I won't be needing it anymore.' He knew that for him, time was almost over and eternity was about to begin, but having trusted Jesus Christ as his Saviour, he knew that his eternity would be with his Lord in heaven.

> *There is a time for everything, and a season for every activity under heaven. A time to be born and a time to die.*
>
> Ecclesiastes 3:1-2

> *He has set eternity in the hearts of men.*
>
> Ecclesiastes 3:11

> *'But God said to him, "You fool! This very night your life will be demanded from you."'*
>
> Luke 12:20

I know whom I have believed, and am convinced that he is able to guard what I have entrusted to him for that day.

2 Timothy 1:12

In human hearts, there is a God-given awareness that there is 'something more' than this transient world. 'He has set eternity in the hearts of men.' If Christ does not return beforehand, then we all have to die. But death is not the end; it is the prelude to eternity and, for the believer, an eternity that will be spent with Christ in heaven. Commit your soul to Christ and you are in safe hands for time and eternity.

FAITH

One Sunday, as a visiting preacher, Pat and I were kindly entertained by friends who insisted that we had a piece of apple pie. Apparently, this was no ordinary apple pie, because the previous day, our hosts had travelled over twenty miles to a bakery where, in their words, 'they make apple pies to die for'. We willingly accepted their invitation and we were not disappointed. The apple pie was delicious.

But, how did we prove the apple pie to be delicious? By just listening to the warm recommendation given by our friends? No, we only proved the quality of the apple pie by tasting it for ourselves.

> *Jesus declared, "I am the bread of life, he who comes to me will never go hungry, and he who believes in me will never be thirsty."*
>
> John 6:35

> *"I am the living bread that came down from heaven. If anyone eats of this bread, he will live for ever."*
>
> John 6:51

> *Taste and see that the LORD is good; blessed is the man who takes refuge in him.*
>
> Psalm 34:8

Jesus is the One Who satisfies, the One Who gives eternal life, but we can only prove it to be so when we personally trust Him for ourselves. There are many who will debate Him, scrutinise Him, criticise Him, but only those who trust Him as their Saviour experience the wonder of His salvation. We have to 'taste' and it is then we 'see that the LORD is good'.

FALL OF MAN

'Do not put the suitcases back in the garage loft until I am there to help you.' These were the clear instructions of my wife as we returned from our holiday in Scotland. That evening I obeyed, but in the morning, I took matters into my own hands.

I climbed the ladder in the garage, put the suitcases back in the loft but then, as I descended, I fell and crashed to the floor. 'Help, Pat, I've fallen,' I cried – and the result, a badly dislocated, broken wrist which required surgery. Oh, the pain and misery because I disobeyed my wife!

> *And the LORD God commanded the man, "You are free to eat from any tree in the garden; but you must not eat from the tree of the knowledge of good and evil."*
>
> Genesis 2:16-17

> *...she [the woman] took some and ate it. She also gave some to her husband, who was with her, and he ate it.*
>
> Genesis 3:6

> *"Because you [...] ate fruit from the tree about which I commanded you, 'You must not eat from it,'*
> *Cursed is the ground because of you;*
> *through painful toil you will eat from it*
> *all the days of your life. [...]*

By the sweat of your brow,
* you will eat your food*
until you return to the ground,
* since from it you were taken;*
for dust you are
* and to dust you will return. "*

Genesis 3:17,19

I was foolish to disobey my wife but to disobey God is utter madness. People often wonder why this world is as it is, and the answer is to be found in Genesis chapter 3. Adam fell into sin and this has resulted in a broken world and a dislocated society. And that is why today we have 'man at enmity with God', 'man at war with man' and 'creation groaning'. There is no other explanation. Oh, the misery and pain brought upon the human race because Adam disobeyed his Maker and fell into sin.

GOSPEL (I)

For many years, Employment Exchanges / Jobcentres issued the British Visitor's Passport (BVP) on behalf of the Passport Office. It was a single-page cardboard document, valid for one year, and could be obtained on sight of an applicant's birth certificate.

One day, 'Ricky', a cockney, was on 'passport' duty when an elderly man arrived with his application form, photograph and birth certificate. As he was leaving, he asked Ricky, 'Do I need a jab?' This was a reasonable question as inoculations were necessary for travel to certain countries. Being a cockney, Ricky thought the man was asking, 'Do I need a job?' His response was unequivocal. 'A jab? What do you need a jab for? You are on holiday, aren't you? Just go and enjoy yourself.'

> *Jesus said, "The Kingdom of God is near. Repent and believe the good news."*
>
> Mark 1:15

> *"Therefore let all Israel be assured of this: God has made this Jesus, whom you crucified, both Lord and Christ." When the people heard this, they were cut to the heart and said to Peter and the other apostles, "Brothers, what shall we do?" Peter replied, "Repent and be baptised, every one of you, in the name of Jesus Christ for the*

forgiveness of your sins. And you will receive the gift of the Holy Spirit."

Acts 2:36-38

"I preached that they should repent and turn to God and prove their repentance by their deeds."

Acts 26:20

The biblical gospel cannot be preached without repentance being emphasised, and yet some seek to do that. They offer a therapeutic Jesus who can make sinners happy, not a crucified Jesus Who died to make them holy. But our hearts need to be jabbed, cut, convicted of sin before we can ever truly trust Jesus as Saviour. And it is then our deeds which prove the reality of our repentance.

GOSPEL (II)

An ornithophobic has a fear of birds, and though I do not quite fall into that category, nevertheless I do panic when a bird flies into the house. Hot summer days and open windows are an open invitation to our feathered friends. And this I discovered when, on entering my study, I came face to face with a startled blackbird. In truth, I was probably more startled than the blackbird.

The bird flew downstairs, whilst I secreted myself in the study and shouted for Pat to take charge. She immediately opened the front door but the frightened bird was not for moving in that direction. Instead, at first, it headed for the bathroom and bedroom windows and was in danger of stunning itself. Several minutes were to pass before, eventually finding the door, the bird flew away to freedom. Panic over for bird and for me!

Jesus said:

> *"I am the door. If anyone enters by Me, he shall be saved."*
>
> John 10:9 (NKJV)

Jesus said:

> *"If the Son sets you free, you will be free indeed."*
>
> John 8:36

Jesus Christ is the door to eternal freedom – freedom from the punishment, the power and ultimately the presence of sin. Sadly, in their search for freedom, people can spend years 'banging their heads against a brick wall' without ever coming to Christ. But He is the way – the only way to freedom. He is the door – the only door to God and to heaven.

GOSPEL (III)

Pat and I were courting and had taken a day trip by train to Dumfries. It was a sunny July afternoon and what could be better than a boat ride on the River Nith? We paid the boatman and I took the oars. 'Do you know what you are doing?' asked a nervous Pat. 'Of course I do,' was my response, keen to impress my fiancée.

'The truth will out' and it did not take too long to emerge. As we drifted ever further from the bank and headed towards the river bridge, the boatman began to gesticulate. He then came at speed towards us shouting, 'You should have told me you didn't know how to row.' Attaching a rope to the boat, he towed us to safety, and the young man who got out of the boat was much humbler than the confident man who had got into the boat.

> *Then Peter got down out of the boat, walked on the water and came towards Jesus. But when he saw the wind, he was afraid and, beginning to sink, cried out, "Lord save me!"*
>
> Matthew 14:29-30

Jesus said:

> *"...the Son of Man came to seek and to save what was lost."*
>
> Luke 19:10

'Are you saved?' was a question I remember being asked as a teenager but not a question that is often asked today.

Are you a Christian? Are you converted? These are perhaps the equivalent questions being asked today. And yet, it is this question 'Are you saved?' that emphasises our true condition.

Our situation is much more desperate than even being saved from drowning. We have rebelled against God, broken His commandments and are heading for judgment – we desperately need to be saved. And that is what Jesus came to do. He left heaven for earth, became a man and went to the cross, all because He loved us and desired to save us from our sins. Have we thanked Him and trusted Him as our Saviour?

GOSPEL (IV)

S hortly after having moved house, it was dark and I turned one evening into what I thought was the driveway of our new home. Something seemed rather unfamiliar, and this was confirmed when the door was opened by a somewhat puzzled gentleman. I had driven not into my driveway but that of my neighbour. Realising I had gone wrong, I had to reverse before I could negotiate my own driveway. An embarrassing lesson was learned that night, that whilst there were many driveways down the road, only one led to my house.

> *There is a way that seems right to a man but in the end it leads to death.*
>
> Proverbs 14:12

> *"...small is the gate and narrow the road that leads to life, and only a few find it."*
>
> Matthew 7:14

> *Jesus answered, "I am the way [...] no one comes to the Father except through me."*
>
> John 14:6

> *"Salvation is found in no one else, for there is no other name under heaven, given to men by which we must be saved."*
>
> Acts 4:12

Many ways to God? Many roads to heaven? That is the mantra of many at the present time, but the Bible is quite explicit. There is only one way to our heavenly home and that is through repentance and faith in Jesus Christ. To some, other ways might seem attractive, even logical, but they are destined to end in death and disappointment. It is only the narrow road 'that leads to life'.

GOSPEL (V)

The doorbell rings and on a spring morning, I am greeted by a tramp – not an unusual sight in the 1980s. However, this 'man of the road' comes with an interesting request. Having given him a drink and a snack, he asks whether my wife has any buttons which she can sew onto his jacket. He explains he is making his way to the Lake District, looking for hotel work, and he wants to be smart and tidy.

Pat finds some buttons and though the 'fragrance' coming from the jacket is somewhat overpowering, she manages to complete the repair job. Minutes later, the man continues his journey, replenished and with new buttons on his jacket. Sadly, his appearance and clothing are such that I cannot imagine the man being acceptable to any prospective employer.

> *All of us have become like one who is unclean,*
> *and all our righteous acts are like filthy rags.*
> Isaiah 64:6

The Bible does not suggest that all our good works, our righteous acts, are of no value, but they are worthless where acceptance with God is concerned. The righteousness of Christ and His death for sinners upon the cross are the only grounds for our acceptance with a holy God. Otherwise, our very best deeds are nothing more than putting 'buttons' upon a filthy jacket.

HEAVEN (I)

My father was a station master and therefore a proportion of my childhood was spent on railway stations. An early memory is of trains stopping at Bare Lane station and a number of wicker baskets being taken out of the guard's van. On the platform, the baskets were opened and a cloud of pigeons took off into the sky. These were homing pigeons, entered by pigeon fanciers into races, and were now beginning their journey home. Quite a sight for a young boy to see.

Noah was told:

> *"Two of every kind of bird, of every kind of animal and of every kind of creature that moves along the ground will come to you to be kept alive."*
>
> Genesis 6:20

Noah did not have to search for the birds and the animals – they simply arrived at the ark by a homing instinct, surely an instinct implanted in homing pigeons today.

David said:

> *I will dwell in the house of the LORD for ever.*
>
> Psalm 23:6

Paul said:

*I am torn between the two: I desire to depart and
be with Christ, which better by far; but it is more
necessary for you that I remain in the body.*
Philippians 1: 23-24

The believer has a homing instinct for heaven. There are
many things on earth which bring us pleasure and
satisfaction, but here we can never find true fulfilment. As
David the Psalmist said:

> *...you will fill me with joy in your presence, with
> eternal pleasures at your right hand.*
Psalm 16:11

Now we have fellowship with and enjoy the presence of
our fellow believers, but in heaven we will have communion
with Christ and enjoy His immediate presence.

HEAVEN (II)

In 2005, we moved into a house which had been specially adapted for our handicapped son. Moving from a small terraced house to a detached house made caring for him so much easier. Walls had been knocked down, doors widened, a ramp and overhead hoists installed, and a sensory garden designed. It was Aaron's house and fully met his needs.

Jesus said:

> *"In my Father's house are many rooms; if it were not so, I would have told you. I am going there to prepare a place for you."*
>
> John 14:2

Jesus could just have said to His disciples, 'I am going there to prepare a place,' but he added 'for you'. He made it personal because heaven will meet and satisfy all our needs. Prepared by Christ, our eternal home will be perfect because Christ Himself is perfect.

Heaven (III)

We had a Blue Badge for Aaron's Motability vehicle, and when it needed renewing, we made an application to the County Council. The replacement came, but within weeks, I detected that the ink on the badge was starting to fade. This did not pose a problem until I received a parking ticket because the details were ineligible.

I appealed against the decision but got short shrift from the parking company who assured me that Blue Badges do not fade. I contacted the County Council and received an apologetic response. They had never known it happen before, but the ink used on a batch of Blue Badges had proved faulty and had resulted in numerous complaints.

The council asked for details of the parking company and subsequently the parking ticket was rescinded. Disappointingly, I heard nothing from the parking company, who had all but accused me of tampering with the Blue Badge.

Jesus said:

> *"Do not store up for yourselves treasures on earth where moth and rust destroy [...] But store up for yourselves treasures in heaven, where moth and rust do not destroy."*
>
> Matthew 6:19-20

...what is seen is temporary, but what is unseen is eternal.

2 Corinthians 4:18

...an inheritance that can never perish, spoil or fade [...] kept in heaven for you, who through faith are shielded by God's power until the coming of the salvation that is ready to be revealed in the last time.

1 Peter 1:4-5

'Change and decay in all around I see'[1]... On earth, that is true of all our possessions, even our prized possessions. With the passing of time, everything perishes, spoils or fades. But what characterises earth does not characterise heaven. Our reward, our inheritance – Jesus and His salvation – that will never change or decay. It will be fresh and new, bright and shining throughout the eternal ages.

Fading is the worldling's pleasure
All his boasted pomp and show;
Solid joys and lasting treasure
None but Zion's children know.

John Newton (1725-1807)

---

[1] *Abide with Me;* Henry Francis Lyte (1793-1847)

Heaven (IV)

Forty years had passed by since we had last bought and sold a house, and estate agents in 2018 were unrecognisable from what they were in 1978. In those far-off days, estate agents did not have websites and the publicity material was very basic – not much more than typed particulars with small photographs glued onto a piece of cardboard.

Today things are very different. Every house merits a professionally produced brochure with stunning images, skilfully drawn floor plans and a narrative designed to grab the attention of any prospective buyer. Indeed, when our house went on the market and we received the brochure, I scarcely recognised it. I commented to Pat, 'Why ever are we selling? Who would want to move from a house and garden as beautiful as this?'

The buzz phrase today is a 'forever home' – a house so perfect that it is where the person intends to live for the rest of their lives. Strangely, I have met people who have bought their 'forever home', but within years, the 'forever' has become 'temporary' and the search for the 'ideal' home has recommenced.

> *For here we do not have an enduring city, but we are looking for the city that is to come.*
>
> Hebrews 13:14

"Father, I want those you have given me to be with me where I am, and to see my glory."

John 17:24

I will dwell in the house of the LORD for ever.

Psalm 23:6

And so we will be with the Lord for ever.

1 Thessalonians 4:17

The only truly 'forever home' is the one provided by Christ in heaven for those who have trusted Him on earth as Saviour. It is a home we cannot move from and never would want to move from because it is perfect. For the real attraction of heaven is not just the absence of pain and sorrow but the immediate presence of Christ. Heaven is to be 'with me' and that is why it will be our 'forever home'.

Far from a world of grief and sin
With God eternally shut in.

Charles Wesley (1707-88)

HOLINESS OF GOD

S ince moving into our retirement home, Pat has insisted that my shoes or trainers are taken off in the hallway and replaced by a pair of slippers. No dirt or dust may be brought in from the outside, and yet, strangely, this is a requirement confined to me and not to other visitors to our home!

> *God said, "Take off your sandals, for the place where you are standing is holy ground."*
>
> Exodus 3:5

Many faiths, as a sign of reverence, still perform their acts of worship barefooted. Just as men today might remove their hats before attending a Christian place of worship, so there are those who remove their shoes. It is a recognition of God's holiness but also of man's sinfulness. Whilst we may not physically remove our shoes, we must not miss the spiritual application. God is a holy God and we dare not come into His Presence carelessly, with unconfessed sin in our hearts.

HUMILITY (I)

No dishwashers in the 1950s or 1960s – and so 'washing up' was a daily chore in every household. As young boys, it was not a task my brother and I warmed to but nevertheless a task which, from time to time, we were expected to perform. The contentious issue was who was going to wash and who was going to wipe? And for some reason, washing the dishes always seemed to be the preferred option. Consequently, 'Whose turn is it to wash and whose turn is it to wipe?' often became a source of disagreement.

> *[Jesus] poured water into a basin and began to wash his disciples' feet, drying them with the towel that was wrapped round him.*
>
> John 13:5

> *Christ Jesus: who, being in very nature God, did not consider equality with God something to be grasped but made himself nothing, taking the very nature of a servant, being made in human likeness.*
>
> Philippians 2:6-7

Feet exposed to sand and dust became dirty, uncomfortable and needed to be washed. This was a menial task, undertaken by servants, but Jesus did not leave or delegate this task to His disciples. He discharged it Himself – no question as to who would do the washing or who would do the wiping. Jesus, even though He was God Incarnate, did both, and in so doing set before us the example of humble service.

Am I prepared to do the menial task, or are there some things I consider to be 'beneath me'?

> *Your attitude should be the same as that of Christ Jesus.*
>
> Philippians 2:5

I must trust Christ as my Saviour but then follow Him as my example.

HUMILITY (II)

On *Your Doorstep* is a monthly magazine delivered to our home and is a directory of the various trades and services available in the area. And so, if you want your carpets cleaned, your garden tidied, your dog walked or even a loft extension, *On Your Doorstep* gives the contact details of reputable people and firms.

Helpfully, on a number of the adverts there are the words 'No job too small'. This is helpful, as it is a common complaint that many firms are only interested in 'major works' and not in small jobs.

> *"...whoever wants to become great among you must be your servant, and whoever wants to be first must be your slave – just as the Son of Man did not come to be served, but to serve, and to give his life as a ransom for many."*
>
> Matthew 20:26-27

> *"Now that I, your Lord and Teacher, have washed your feet, you also should wash one another's feet. I have set you an example that yo u should do as I have done for you."*
>
> John 13:14-15

As those who seek to follow the example of Jesus, our motto must also be 'no job too small', 'no task too menial', 'no chore beneath me'. Sadly, pride can so easily creep in and 'thinking of ourselves more highly than we ought'

(Romans 12:3), we hesitate to do work that might require our hands to get dirty.

> *Teach me, my God and King*
> *In all things Thee to see;*
> *And what I do in anything,*
> *To do it as for Thee.*
>
> *A servant with this clause*
> *Makes drudgery divine;*
> *Who sweeps a room, as for Thy laws*
> *Makes that and the action fine.*
>
> George Herbert (1593-1632)

HYPOCRISY (I)

A young man, well known to me, came into the Jobcentre, desperate for any kind of work. This was a pleasant surprise because when I had interviewed him in the past, he had shown no appetite for work. He assured me that he was prepared to 'consider anything' and I arranged for him to be interviewed for work as a builder's labourer. He got the job and I rejoiced at his change of heart and my success in getting him into employment.

My joy, however, was short-lived, as browsing through the local paper a few weeks later, I read that this man had been in court charged with a serious offence. The judge was of a mind to send him to prison but having heard from his defence lawyer, he had decided on a suspended prison sentence.

Why this change of heart? The lawyer explained that his client, having been unemployed for almost two years, had at last obtained work and was now able to support his family. For this reason, he pleaded with the judge not to impose a custodial sentence. Shortly afterwards, having deceived both me and the judge, the man gave up his job and once again signed on for benefits.

> *"The LORD does not look on the things that man looks at. Man looks at the outward appearance but the LORD looks at the heart."*
>
> 1 Samuel 16:7

Do not be deceived: God cannot be mocked. A man reaps what he sows.

Galatians 6:7

Nothing in all creation is hidden from God's sight. Everything is uncovered and laid bare before the eyes of him to whom we must give account.

Hebrews 4:13

We can be deceived. The 'wool can be pulled over our eyes', but that can never be the case with God. He sees right through the excuses, the pretence, the hypocrisy – He knows the 'real' me, the real 'you'. He knows whether I am truly sorry for my sin and if my repentance is sincere. The Lord is omniscient, and therefore He is the only Judge whose verdict will be fair and indisputable.

HYPOCRISY (II)

It was Remembrance Sunday and suddenly the solemnity of the occasion was broken by a deafening noise. A man in the gallery had left his seat, stamped down the stairs and slammed both an inner door and outer door of the church. The man was a pacifist and had taken great exception to the minister saying it was 'a glorious thing to die in war'.

Irrespective of the rights or wrongs of what the minister was saying, it seemed a strange way for a pacifist to make his protest. I would have expected a 'man of peace' to have registered his objection in a less aggressive and a gentler way.

After I had preached at a Sunday evening service, we all participated in the Lord's Supper. Within minutes, an 'unholy' sound was coming from a side room, as church officers, with raised voices, tore into one another. Having just 'examined ourselves' in the presence of the Lord, such behaviour was surely inconsistent and hypocritical.

> *Out of the same mouth come praise and cursing.*
> *My brothers, these things should not be.*
>
> James 3:10

At times, we all stand accused of hypocrisy and inconsistency, and the Bible is right: 'these things should not be'. Whenever I am tempted to lie or gossip, to be bitter or jealous, to belittle or humiliate another person, may I remember these words of James. The unconverted world is watching and they will soon observe any disparity between my profession and my behaviour.

JESUS AS JUDGE

For a number of years I was umpire for Ingleton Cricket Club in the Westmorland Cricket League. I tried to be scrupulously fair but all umpires are human and I certainly made wrong decisions. I remember giving a batsman out caught and the player seemed most unhappy. As he walked back to the pavilion, a number of Ingleton fielders conceded that the batsman had played the ball into the ground before it had been caught.

I made the decision in good faith but it was undoubtedly the wrong decision. I later apologised to the batsman, and he graciously accepted that I had made a genuine mistake. That was one error I knew about – how many more did I make that I knew nothing about?

> *...the Father judges no one but has entrusted all judgment to the Son.*
>
> John 5:22

> *...judge nothing before the appointed time; wait till the Lord comes. He will bring to light what is hidden in darkness and will expose the motives of men's hearts.*
>
> 1 Corinthians 4:5

How reassuring that Jesus Christ – no human being – will be our Judge. As man and God, He will be unbiased, and being omniscient, He will be in possession of all the facts. No miscarriages of justice, no need for appeals or retrials – the 'Judge of all the earth' (Genesis 18:25) will do right.

JUDGEMENT

Towards the end of my time in the civil service, I was invited to have a 'jar' with the manager. However, this was not a convivial, friendly drink – it was something more serious. It was a Job Appraisal Review where one's performance over the past twelve months was assessed.

> ...we will all stand before God's judgment seat [...] So then, each of us will give an account of himself to God.
>
> Romans 14:10,12

> ...we must all appear before the judgment seat of Christ, that each one may receive what is due to him, for the things done while in the body, whether good or bad.
>
> 2 Corinthians 5:10

Believers as well as unbelievers will stand before the judgment seat of Christ. This is evident from the words of the Apostle Paul. He does not say 'you' or 'they'; he says, '...we must all appear before the judgment seat of Christ.' He says 'we', and in so doing, he includes himself. However, for the Christian, the judgment will not be to establish his eternal destiny; it will rather be to evaluate his deeds. Was I motivated by self-interest or was my chief aim the glory of God?

MAN

Our daughter and family were away for the weekend in London, and we had agreed to look after the guinea pig. On the Friday morning, I noticed Pat was clearing my desk. 'What are you doing?' I enquired. 'That is where the guinea pig is going,' was the response. My mild protest was to no avail, and I had to accept that for three days I was below Daisy in the pecking order.

My daughter bought a Boston terrier puppy, and though not a dog lover, Desmond had soon won me over. However, I have to admit to being astonished when I visited the local pet store. Advent calendars for cats. Flat caps for dogs. And almost anything you can buy for a baby, you can also buy for a pet. I did not know whether to laugh or cry!

> *When God created man, he made him in the likeness of God. He created them male and female and blessed them.*
>
> Genesis 5:1-2

> *The LORD God had formed out of the ground all the beasts of the field and all the birds of the air. He brought them to the man to see what he would name them; and whatever the man called each living creature, that was its name.*
>
> Genesis 2:19

> *What is man that you are mindful of him, the son of man that you care for him? You made him a*

little lower than the heavenly beings and
crowned him with glory and honour. You made
him ruler over the works of your hands; you put
everything under his feet: all flocks and herds,
and the beasts of the field, the birds of the air and
the fish of the sea.

Psalm 8:4-8

Animals are God's creation, a source of great pleasure, and should never be ill-treated. But it is man who is the crown of God's creation. Increasingly, this is being forgotten, with man being seen as just another animal. It is man alone who has the capacity to know and worship God because he has been made in God's image and after God's likeness. It is indeed a back-to-front world when some would rather worship a d-o-g than worship G-o-d.

ORIGINAL SIN

My son told me the first two words spoken by our youngest granddaughter, after the usual 'mummy' and 'daddy'. And they were significant words. She picked up a toy, held it tightly to her chest and then, when approached by her older siblings, said, 'Mine. Mine.' But, when her siblings picked up their toys, she marched over to them and said, 'Share. Share.'

> *Surely I was sinful at birth, from the time my mother conceived me.*
>
> Psalm 51:5

There is an attractive innocence about young children, and yet they are still born with a sinful nature. Jealousy, envy, selfishness are not vices which have to be taught; they are inherent in every human being. How sad this biblical truth is so often denied and youngsters are not given the discipline and guidance they require.

PRESENCE OF GOD

It was a great honour for Pat to be invited to a garden party at Buckingham Palace and an honour for me to accompany her. It was over twenty-five years since we had last visited London, and we knew that travelling by Tube to our accommodation on Drury Lane would be for us 'country yokels' a considerable challenge.

Arriving at King's Cross station, we bought tickets for Covent Garden but were somewhat disorientated by the hustle and bustle of our capital city. We made our way to the appropriate platform and Pat approached a well-dressed man. 'Can you help us?' she said. 'We are from the Yorkshire Dales and want a train to Covent Garden.' The man, a solicitor from South Africa, could not have been more helpful, telling us to 'stick with him' as he would be alighting at Holborn Street, the previous station.

He advised Pat to conceal her purse as this was London, not the Yorkshire Dales, and within minutes, we boarded the train together. We chatted, and then to our delight and slight embarrassment, he did not get off at Holborn Street but got off with us at Covent Garden and escorted us to our accommodation on Drury Lane. What a lovely man, and he literally 'went out of his way' to help us.

The LORD replied, "My Presence will go with you and I will give you rest." Then Moses said to

*him, "If your Presence does not go with us, do
not send us up from here."*

Exodus 33:14-15

*After the death of Moses [...] the LORD said to
Joshua [...] "As I was with Moses, so I will be
with you; I will never leave you nor forsake
you."*

Joshua 1:1,5

*I am always with you; you hold me by my right
hand. You guide me with your counsel and
afterwards you will take me into glory.*

Psalm 73:23-24

*"And surely, I am with you always, to the very
end of the age."*

Matthew 28:20

The believer is on a journey from earth to heaven – a
journey which can be fraught with dangers and difficulties.
But we are never on our own. That which was experienced
by Moses, Joshua and the Psalmist during the days of their
pilgrimage has been promised to every child of God. His
Presence and His counsel will go with us. What a comfort
and encouragement to know that we have a Guide and a
Friend who accompanies us every step of the way.

PROVIDENCE OF GOD

My grandfather, and to a lesser extent my grandmother, were cat lovers, and I cannot remember a time when there was not a feline in their home. A variety of 'moggies' including a tortoiseshell, a Manx cat without a tail and even a cat with three legs were all long-term residents.

Grandmother was not sentimental about animals, and I can recall cold winter nights with cats purring in front of an open fire – or they were until half-past eight. Then Grandmother would unceremoniously get hold of the cats and put them out of the back door. No cat slept overnight in her house.

My grandparents lived on a busy road and, inevitably, there were cats which fell victim to the traffic. My grandfather coming across any dead cat would pick it up and bring it home to be buried. A small area of his garden became a cats' cemetery.

> *"Are not two sparrows sold for a penny? Yet not one of them will fall to the ground apart from the will of your Father. And even the very hairs of your head are all numbered. So don't be afraid; you are worth more than many sparrows."*
>
> Matthew 10:29-31

> *"Are not five sparrows sold for two pennies? Yet not one of them is forgotten by God."*
>
> Luke 12:6

93

The concern which Grandfather had for cats is but a pale shadow of the concern which God has for all His creation. Sparrows, we would say, are 'two a penny' but they are still the objects of His care. How much more are believers – made in His image, redeemed by His Son – objects of His care and watchfulness? The very hairs of our head are all numbered and are of some value to Him. Let us rejoice that we have such a Father in heaven.

Resurrection of Jesus

(I)

For a couple of years, I had been Vice Chair of Governors at a school for multi-handicapped children. It was a demanding position but made much easier by the competence and expertise of the Chair of Governors. It was, therefore, a great shock when I received a phone call from the headteacher to say that this well-respected man had collapsed and died.

A week later, it was a solemn group of men and women who met for their appointed meeting and poignantly saw an empty chair. I started the meeting by asking the governors to stand for a minute's silence, as we fondly remembered our departed friend. It was a sombre occasion and not without tears.

> *...the Lord Jesus, on the night in which he was betrayed, took bread, and when he had given thanks, he broke it and said, "This is my body, which is for you; do this in remembrance of me." In the same way, after supper, he took the cup saying, "This cup is the new covenant in my blood; do this, whenever you drink it, in remembrance of me."*
>
> 1 Corinthians 11:23-25

Jesus our Lord [...] He was delivered over to death for our sins and was raised to life for our justification.

Romans 4:24-25

When we meet at the Lord's Table, we do not meet to remember a dead friend; we rather meet to remember a Saviour Who was dead but is now alive for evermore. That means there is solemnity but also rejoicing because the One we remember, though absent in body, is present in spirit. And at His coming, we shall see His physical form again.

Lifted up was He to die,
'It is finished!' was His cry;
Now in heaven exalted high;
Hallelujah! What a Saviour.

When He comes, our glorious King;
All His ransomed home to bring,
Then anew this song we'll sing:
Hallelujah! What a Saviour.

Philip Paul Bliss (1838-1876)

Resurrection of Jesus

(II)

As a child, our daughter had numerous pets – hamsters, gerbils, guinea pigs – which brought her great happiness. The downside was the grief she experienced whenever one of the animals died. One morning she had gone to school when I noticed that a recently bought gerbil was not breathing. We had a burial, and then I went to the pet shop in Settle and bought an almost identical gerbil. On her return from school, we waited with bated breath but thankfully Joanna did not detect it was a different gerbil and a 'time of mourning' was prevented. It was many, many years later before I made her aware of our deceit.

> [Jesus] began to teach them that the Son of Man must suffer many things and be rejected by the elders, chief priests and teachers of the law, and that he must be killed and after three days rise again. He spoke plainly about this.
>
> Mark 8: 31-32

> The angel said to the women, "Do not be afraid, for I know that you are looking for Jesus, who

was crucified. He is not here; he has risen, just as he said."

While the women were on their way, some of the guards went into the city and reported to the chief priests everything that had happened. When the chief priests had met with the elders and devised a plan, they gave the soldiers a large sum of money telling them, "You are to say, 'His disciples came during the night and stole him away while we were asleep.'" So the soldiers took the money and did as they were instructed. And this story has been widely circulated among the Jews to this very day.

Matthew 28:11-13,15

Jesus said:

"Do not be afraid. I am the First and the Last. I am the Living One; I was dead, and behold I am alive for ever and ever."

Revelation 1:17-18

He [Christ] committed no sin, and no deceit was found in his mouth.

1 Peter 2:22

With regard to the gerbils, we were – I hope for a justifiable reason – guilty of deceit. But concerning the resurrection of Jesus, the disciples were not guilty of any kind of deceit. The elders, chief priests and soldiers invented a story that the disciples had stolen the body of Jesus. However, the Gospel writer makes it clear that this story was an invention, a concoction on the part of some who, while knowing Jesus had risen from the dead, had no desire to face the truth.

Even more tragic, there have always been those who would accuse Jesus Himself of deceit. They deny His physical resurrection saying, without a shred of evidence, 'He only swooned on the cross,' or, 'He had a twin brother who impersonated Him.' Such myths can easily be refuted, but they make Jesus out to be a liar, a deceiver, because He said He would rise, and had risen, from the dead. 'No deceit was found in his mouth.' Let not the cynics accuse Christ and, in so doing, undermine the wonder of the resurrection, which is the bedrock of the Christian faith.

SATAN (I)

In order to help the household budget, I became a paperboy, and for several years, whatever the weather, I was up at 6am and ready for the morning delivery. The money was not great – twelve shillings a week, I seem to recall – but it was my first taste of work and something which I very much enjoyed.

There was only one downside and that was the likelihood of being bitten by a dog. I was invading their territory and they had every right to retaliate. Dogs outside posed the greater danger, but some dogs were waiting inside, ready to pounce as the paper came through the letterbox. Only hand dexterity sometimes ensured that one finished the round with all fingers still intact.

I was bitten twice, and those experiences as a youngster have caused me to be wary of dogs ever since. The first occasion, a barking mongrel ran at me and bit my leg, whilst on the second occasion, the canine was rather more subtle. This dog was a non-barking corgi and, slowly walking up to me, it unexpectedly sank its teeth into my ankle.

> Your enemy the devil prowls around like a roaring lion looking for someone to devour.
>
> 1 Peter 5:8

> Satan himself masquerades as an angel of light.
>
> 2 Corinthians 11:14

Satan [...] we are not unaware of his schemes.
2 Corinthians 2:11

In parts of the world today, Satan is not barking as a dog but roaring as a lion. Believers are being persecuted, imprisoned, martyred as the devil attacks the body of Christ. In the West, for generations we have been spared such attacks, but there is evidence that Satan now is beginning to bare his teeth.

However, such is his subtlety that the 'roaring lion' can become an 'angel of light'. He introduces false teaching into the church, which is attractive but deceptive, and the undiscerning are led astray. We are back to the Garden of Eden, where the fruit was attractive but Satan used it to deceive Adam and Eve. We must ensure that 'we are not unaware of his schemes'.

SATAN (II)

It was the lunch hour when the relative peace of the office was broken by the shouting and cursing of a drunken man. It was not altogether an unknown experience as men having over-imbibed at the pub sometimes went to the Jobcentre / Benefits Office to try to recoup their losses. This man was especially obnoxious, and when he began to threaten the staff, we had no alternative but to send for the police.

In the office, there was a joiner, apparently minding his own business, repairing a faulty window. As the swearing and threats continued, this workman climbed down from his ladder, walked across the floor and planted a right uppercut on the chin of the drunken man. He fell as if poleaxed. The joiner, without saying a word, climbed his ladder and continued his work. Apparently, in his younger days, he had been a champion boxer in the navy.

When the police eventually arrived, they just assumed that the man had slumped to the floor, and getting him to his feet, they dragged him out of the office. The man they took out was certainly quieter and more subdued than the man who had come in.

> *The LORD God said to the serpent [...] "I will put enmity between you and the woman, and between your offspring and hers; he will crush your head, and you will strike his heel."*
>
> Genesis 3:14-15

The God of peace will soon crush Satan under your feet.

Romans 16:20

And the devil, who deceived them, was thrown into the lake of burning sulphur, where the beast and the false prophet had been thrown. They will be tormented day and night for ever and ever.

Revelation 20:10

Satan is a powerful foe but never forget he is a defeated foe. He is not as powerful as once he was, because on the cross, Jesus bruised his head. Therefore, whilst we do not underestimate his power, neither do we overestimate it. Jesus is the Victor and Satan's fate is certain.

SATAN (III)

The summer house had stood for thirteen years at the bottom of the garden and had been enjoyed by family and friends – an oasis of quietness where I could read, or a make-believe café where the grandchildren could play. Sadly, all this was to come to an end one night in March, when we had the visit of the 'Beast from the East' – gusts of freezing Siberian air. So ferocious were the winds that when I looked out of the window the following morning, the summer house had collapsed like a pack of cards and the roof was in the garden next door. It had not been able to withstand the 'Beast from the East'.

> *Jesus said, "Simon, Simon, Satan has asked to sift you as wheat. But I have prayed for you, Simon, that your faith may not fail."*
>
> Luke 22:31-32

> *Put on the full armour of God, so that you can take your stand against the devil's schemes. For our struggle is not against flesh and blood, but against the rulers, against the authorities, against the powers of this dark world and against the spiritual forces of evil in the heavenly realms. Therefore put on the full armour of God, so that when the day of evil comes, you may be able to stand your ground, and after you have done everything, to stand.*
>
> Ephesians 6:10-13

Satan is not the 'Beast from the East' but rather the 'beast from hell'. He wants us back, ever seeking to destroy the saving faith which the believer has in Christ. He need not succeed because God Himself has provided all the resources necessary to repel him. It is as we put on 'the full armour of God' that we are able to 'take [our] stand against the devil's schemes'.

SATAN (IV)

The first radio programme I can ever recall hearing was the 1950s comedy *Educating Archie*. It was hugely popular and surprisingly so because it was a ventriloquist act on the radio. To me, as a boy, Archie Andrews was a real person, not a dummy being operated by Peter Brough. I understand that up to fifteen million listeners tuned in weekly to the Light Programme to hear of his escapades.

Jesus said:

> *"You belong to your father, the devil, and you want to carry out your father's desires. He was a murderer from the beginning, not holding to the truth, for there is no truth in him. When he lies, he speaks his native language, for he is a liar and the father of lies."*
>
> John 8:44-45

> *Satan himself masquerades as an angel of light. It is not surprising, then, if his servants also masquerade as servants of righteousness.*
>
> 2 Corinthians 11:14-15

As a ventriloquist speaks through a dummy, so Satan can speak through men and women. Although they are personally responsible for what they say, nevertheless they are being motivated by the devil. That is why when Peter said he would never allow Jesus to go to the cross, his

106

Master answered, "Get behind me, Satan!" (Matthew 16:23). Jesus recognised who was speaking.

This was something I had to remember when preaching in the open air and faced with obscenity and blasphemy. However appalled and outraged I felt, I needed to tell myself they were only, to paraphrase John's Gospel, 'carrying out their father's desires'. I hope this caused me to be forthright but, at the same time, compassionate.

SECOND COMING OF

CHRIST (I)

I am sure that all banks today have a wide array of security systems, but in the 1960s, things were not quite as sophisticated. At the sub branch, we pressed a button, a light flashed and the alarm sounded. The system was tested monthly, although there were occasions when it went off unintentionally.

What was the response of passers-by to the alarm going off? The truth was: no response. No one ever telephoned the police or took any kind of action. People just assumed it was a practice or a false alarm and so continued shopping or whatever else they happened to be doing.

> *...in the last days scoffers will come, scoffing and following their own evil desires. They will say, "Where is this 'coming' he promised? Ever since our fathers died, everything goes on as it has since the beginning of creation."*
>
> 2 Peter 3:3-5

Warnings are given in Scripture and the alarm is constantly sounded by preachers, but they are ignored by the majority of people. 'God will not intervene. Jesus will not come again. There will be no Day of Judgment.' That is the general consensus. We have been warned about these things but they have not happened in the past – why should we expect them to happen in the future?

How we need to understand that no alarm in Scripture is a false alarm. True, we do not know the timing, but we do know every warning will be fulfilled. God will intervene. Jesus will return. We shall be judged. Are we ready and prepared for these momentous events?

SECOND COMING OF

CHRIST (II)

I have in my possession a photograph which rarely sees the light of day. It is the 1954 crowning of the Bare Methodist Church Sunday School queen, with attendants and page boys. The two page boys with silk shirts and short back and sides haircuts are me and my six-year-old twin brother. Not a photograph I rush to share with family and friends!

However, I have another similar photograph which tells a very different story. It is 1984 and my daughter Joanna is in the retinue as the Ingleton Gala queen is crowned. A special occasion for her and for me – so special that we delayed until evening our holiday departure for Scotland.

> ...*when our Lord Jesus comes with all his holy ones.*
>
> 1 Thessalonians 3:13

> ...*we believe that Jesus died and rose again, and so we believe that God will bring with Jesus those who have fallen asleep in him.*
>
> 1 Thessalonians 4:14

> *See the Lord is coming with thousands upon thousands of his holy ones.*
>
> Jude 14

110

Believers will accompany Christ. They will be part of His retinue when He returns to this earth. Today, like Him, we are often despised and rejected, but at His Second Coming we will have a status and honour which we never had on earth. On that day, there will be no embarrassment for the believer – just pure unadulterated joy.

SELF-DECEPTION

A Friday evening in July and the doorbell rings. On the step is a distressed man and we immediately invite him in. He has a tragic, if rather an improbable, tale to tell. Having come over from France, he is due to attend a course at Lancaster University on Monday.

Four weeks ago, his wife died suddenly and though he did not feel like attending the course, his friends have encouraged him to do so. However, in his sorrowful sate, he has not sorted out his finances, and though money is waiting for him at the bank on Monday, he has no money for the weekend.

As he tells his tale of woe, he weeps real tears and then asks if we can pray about the situation. This we do and as the man pours his heart to the Lord, he prays with passion. He also explains how important it is for him to have fellowship with believers, and he wants to know what time the services are on Sunday.

Eventually the inevitable question comes: can I lend him some money which he will definitely repay? To say I 'smell a rat' would be an understatement, but knowing what the Bible says about 'entertaining angels unawares', I always give such people the benefit of the doubt.

Consequently, I telephone the local youth hostel, and after getting confirmation they have vacancies, I give the man money for an overnight stay. I arrange to meet him next morning outside the youth hostel, and off he goes thanking the Lord for this 'wonderful provision'.

I telephone the youth hostel on the Saturday morning and – surprise, surprise – there has been no sight of the man. Despite this, I still keep the arrangement and he turns up at the allotted time of 8.30am. 'Have you had a good night in the hostel?' I ask mischievously. Not at all taken aback, he tells me another amazing story.

As he had been making his way to the hostel the previous evening, he had got into conversation with a couple who were also Christians. When they heard he was spending the night at the youth hostel, they had insisted he stayed the night with them. 'What were they called and where did they live?' I enquire. He is quite unable to answer either question but is rejoicing that the Lord has met his need.

By now the 'rat' is certainly smelling and I tell my 'friend' I am not in a position to help him any further. The man raises no objection, thanks me for my kindness and assures me he will be at the service in the morning. We shake hands and go our separate ways.

That evening, I feel most guilty when I get a phone call from the vicar of Ingleton. 'John,' he says, 'I want to warn you because I think we might have a conman in the village.' On leaving me, it appears the man then told his tale at the vicarage and left £25 the richer. Several months later, the vicar was contacted by the police as the 'crying conman' had committed offences throughout the country.

> "Not everyone who says to me, 'Lord, Lord,' will enter the kingdom of heaven, but only he who does the will of my Father who is in heaven. Many will say to me on that day, 'Lord, Lord,

did we not prophesy in your name, and in your name, drive out demons and perform many miracles?' Then I will tell you plainly, 'I never knew you. Away from me you evildoers!'"

Matthew 7:21-23

"'These people honour me with their lips, but their hearts are far from me.'"

Matthew 15:8

It is sadly possible to be a fake disciple of Christ – to call Him 'Lord, Lord' without ever really meaning it. True discipleship involves far more than merely invoking the name of Jesus; it demands practical obedience. The conman may have deceived many – even himself – but he is not able to deceive the One Who will be his Judge.

SELF-EXAMINATION (I)

Five minutes past three and the doorbell rings; in your home, nothing to be too concerned about, but in the bank, something which inevitably caused pressure and panic. It could only mean one thing: the inspectors had arrived. In those days, the doors shut at 3pm, and as cashiers, we would just have started to balance our books for the day, but now the tills were taken from us and the money was counted by the inspectors. They were not too concerned, however, as to whether we were £1 over or 10 shillings short – they had greater things in mind.

Were the bags of copper and silver really copper and silver or were they bags of sand and stones? Were the £1, the £5, the £10 notes genuine or were they fake notes? This was their great concern, and it was here that the inspectors put the emphasis. Any fake currency would have been discovered and the dishonest employee exposed.

> *"When the Son of Man comes in his glory, and all the angels with him, he will sit on his throne in heavenly glory. All the nations will be gathered before him, and he will separate the people one from another as a shepherd separates the sheep from the goats. He will put the sheep on his right and the goats on his left."*
>
> Matthew 25:31-33

If we judged ourselves, we would not come under judgment.

1 Corinthians 11:31

Examine yourselves to see whether you are in the faith; test yourselves. Do you not realise that Jesus Christ is in you – unless, of course, you fail the test?

2 Corinthians 13:5

The Great Inspector will return and distinguish the sheep from the goats, the wheat from the chaff, the real from the fake. How important that our faith is real and genuine. Is it not a sobering thought that many who thought they had 'saving' faith will sadly discover it was a 'dead' faith?

There is an urgent need for self-examination. Have I truly repented? Am I trusting Christ alone for salvation? Do I have the inner witness of the Spirit? These are the marks of a genuine saving faith, not of a faith that is dead and spurious.

SELF-EXAMINATION (II)

My daughter enjoyed school but was not over-enthusiastic when it came to PE and games. She was often looking for excuses and the opportunity to take advantage of her occasional asthma attacks. This was particularly so as she got older and when, uncannily, her wheezing always seemed to be worse on a Friday morning. However, she could only be excused if a parental letter was sent to the school.

One Friday I wrote the PE teacher a letter, which I later learned had been pinned on the staff noticeboard. 'Dear Sir. Please can Joanna be excused games today, as she is anticipating an asthma attack around 10.45 this morning.' I think the staff knew precisely what I was trying to say!

> ...on the Sabbath day, he went into the synagogue, as was his custom.
>
> Luke 4:16

> Let us not give up meeting together, as some are in the habit of doing.
>
> Hebrews 10:25

During my thirty years as a pastor, I met a few believers, thankfully not many, who suffered from what I termed 'Sundayitis'. They were always well enough to do what they wanted on other days, but strangely they were afflicted by tiredness or illness on a Sunday. I hope I am not being judgmental but perhaps we all ought to ask the question,

'Are there times when things prevent me from going to church that would not stop me from going anywhere else?'

SIN (I)

Is there a cure for snoring? If so, my wife would be delighted to know it. To my grandchildren, if not to Pat, it is a source of great amusement. And yet, I myself am quite unaware that I do snore because it is something I only do when I am asleep and not conscious.

I do not underestimate the problems associated with snoring, and I know that in the case of two elderly ladies, it caused a breakdown in their relationship. They were sharing a bedroom on holiday when one complained she was being kept awake by the snoring of the other. Her friend objected to this insinuation, assuring her companion, 'I never snore' – a somewhat presumptuous statement to make, I would suggest.

> *If a person sins and does what is forbidden in any of the LORD's commands, even though he does not know it, he is guilty and will be held responsible. He is to bring to the priest as a guilt offering a ram from the flock, one without defect and of the proper value. In this way the priest will make atonement for the wrong he has committed unintentionally, and he will be forgiven.*
>
> Leviticus 5:17-18

> *Who can discern his errors? Forgive my hidden faults.*
>
> Psalm 19:12

Nothing in all creation is hidden from God's sight. Everything is uncovered and laid bare before the eyes of him to whom we must give account.

Hebrews 4:13

...the blood of Jesus, his Son, purifies us from all sin.

1 John 1:7

I can snore without knowing it, but much more seriously, I can sin without knowing it. And, as with snoring, whilst I might be unaware what I am doing, others are only too aware. I might be blind to my pride, my boasting, my bitterness, my jealousy, but others are able to see it. They see the sin being manifested, but it is only God who truly sees the depth and the depravity of my sin.

I have a record by Jim Reeves and it contains these words:

> *Forgive the sins that I confess to Thee.*
> *Forgive those secret sins, I do not even see.*
> C.M. Battersby

This should be our daily prayer for as I confess 'those secret sins, I do not even see', so I have the comfort and assurance of knowing that 'the blood of Jesus, his Son, purifies us [me] from *all* sin'.

120

SIN (II)

Our first home in Ingleton had a small front garden, which was only exposed to the sun for a few hours in the morning. Consequently, it was not easy to grow things, and Pat turned it over into a wild flower garden. One morning, there was a knock on the door, and standing there was our neighbour. 'I've just pulled this up. Japanese knotweed. It will take your garden over.' Pat was not too impressed by this neighbourly interference, but perhaps the man was doing us a favour. Japanese knotweed can grow at an alarming rate, soon overtaking a garden and causing potential damage to tarmac and property.

> *"If your right eye causes you to sin, gouge it out and throw it away. [...] And if your right hand causes you to sin, cut it off and throw it away. It is better for you to lose one part of your body than for your whole body to go into hell."*
> Matthew 5:29-30

> *See to it that no one misses the grace of God and that no bitter root grows up to cause trouble and defile many.*
> Hebrews 12:15

> *Each one is tempted when by his own evil desire, he is dragged away and enticed. Then, after*

desire has conceived, it gives birth to sin; and sin,
when it is full-grown gives birth to death.

James 1:14-15

Sin is nothing to 'play' with, and 'little sins' can very soon grow and become impossible to control. Jesus, in the Sermon on the Mount, emphasised that sin needs drastic action. He did so by the use of vivid language: gouging out eyes and cutting off hands. Jesus was not suggesting that we mutilate our bodies but, recognising the power and effect of sin, encouraging us to take decisive and appropriate action.

Sin (III)

As a pastor in Ingleton, I was frequently asked to countersign passport application forms and photos. On the back of the photo, I had to write, 'I certify that this is a true likeness of—'. Applicants were happy for me to write these words and yet how often they protested. 'Isn't it awful?' 'I don't look like that.' 'That's not me.' But, yes. It was them because the camera cannot lie.

> *The heart is deceitful above all things and beyond cure. Who can understand it?*
>
> Jeremiah 17:9

> *There is no one righteous, not even one; there is no one who understands; there is no one who seeks God.*
>
> Romans 3:10-11

> *"You say, 'I am rich; I have acquired wealth and do not need a thing.' But you do not realise that you are wretched, pitiful, poor, blind and naked."*
>
> Revelation 3:17

The Bible tells us what we are really like and it is not an attractive picture. Therefore, our natural inclination is to say, 'That's not me,' and whilst accepting it might be true of others, we are persuaded 'that is not true of me'. Sadly, it is true that 'the heart is deceitful', 'no one [is] righteous, not even one', 'all have sinned'. The Bible cannot lie and it

123

is only when we have accepted this true diagnosis of our condition that we can then seek for the remedy in Christ.

SIN (IV)

One summer, as a student, I worked for a well-known retail store. My duties chiefly consisted of bringing goods from the warehouse onto the shop floor, and on busy occasions, helping in the cafeteria. However, one morning, I was asked to do something quite different.

Apparently, the sales figures were disappointing, targets were not being met and the manager was under pressure. Consequently, I was told to trawl through back copies of the local paper and underline any article which indicated that visitor numbers were down and money was tight.

Such articles were not in plenteous supply, but there were some and these were passed to the manager. In reporting to head office, he would use these reports as mitigating evidence for disappointing retail figures.

> *Jesus replied: "'Love the Lord your God with all your heart and all your soul and all your mind.' This is the first and greatest commandment. And the second is like it: 'Love your neighbour as yourself.'"*
>
> Matthew 22:37-39

> *...all have sinned and fall short of the glory of God.*
>
> Romans 3:23

For whoever keeps the whole law and yet stumbles at just one point is guilty of breaking all of it.

James 2:10

Jesus said:

"I always do what pleases him."

John 8:29

The standard or the target set by God is perfection – the faultless keeping of all His commands. That target has not and cannot be met by any human being – we have all fallen short of the standard set by God. Some try to excuse themselves by pleading mitigating circumstances, but that does not change the situation. We are all sinners who have missed the target, and therefore, we need a Saviour. And that Saviour can only be the One Who met the target by keeping perfectly all the commandments of God – the One Who died for sinners upon the cross of Calvary. That One can only be the Lord Jesus Christ.

SIN (V)

School assembly on a Wednesday morning was the time when those heading for detention were named. One Wednesday the headmaster decided not only to 'name' the miscreants but also to 'shame' them by reading out their individual offences. Sadly, not a good idea.

As the charges were read out, instead of the 'hush of disgust' which the head had expected, there were instead 'guffaws of laughter'. For some reason 'spitting at a prefect from an upstairs window' brought forth much merriment. Rarely did the headmaster lose his cool, but he did that morning, and abandoning the experiment, he ordered us all to our classrooms.

> *"How then could I do such a wicked thing and sin against God?"*
>
> Genesis 39:9

> *Your eyes are too pure to look on evil; you cannot tolerate wrong.*
>
> Habakkuk 1:13

> *Fools mock at making amends for sin.*
>
> Proverbs 14:9

> *For we must all appear before the judgment seat of Christ, that each one may receive what is due to him for the things done while in the body, whether good or bad.*
>
> 2 Corinthians 5:10

To many, sin is a 'laughing matter', not to be taken too seriously and certainly nothing to worry about. This, however, is not how God sees sin. In His eyes, all sin is vile and loathsome and must be judged. On the Day of Judgment, there will be no mirth or jollity, just the sober realisation that all our words and actions are known to God. Our sin must either be forgiven in Christ or be judged by God.

SOUL

I was driving an elderly lady to a church meeting when she pointed towards a house and exclaimed, 'I don't agree with that.' Her focus was a FOR SALE sign with the words UNDER OFFER emblazoned upon it. 'I think,' she said, 'they should offer what is being asked for and not try to offer less.' Not having the time or energy to explain what the sign really meant, I just nodded in agreement.

> "What good is it for a man to gain the whole world, yet forfeit his soul? Or what can a man give in exchange for his soul?"
>
> Mark 8:36-37

To obtain our souls, Satan offers the world – the world of pleasure or the world of possessions. Sadly, there are many who accept his offer, not realising that they are being short-changed. For even if he could offer the whole world – and he can't – that is way under the true value of the human soul.

Our souls are immortal – they will never ever die – and it is foolish to sell our souls to the devil. They need to be entrusted to Jesus; He died to save our souls, and in His hands they are safe and secure for time and eternity.

SOVEREIGNTY OF GOD

(I)

We were on holiday with my brother and his family near Keswick. The accommodation was adequate but not too spacious for four adults and five children. Most days the weather was wet and trips out were necessary in order to preserve family harmony.

Returning home one evening, with tired and hungry children, we encountered an unexpected problem. We could not find the house key. As the search intensified and the frustration increased, the tenseness was broken by one of the children. 'Can't Margaret Thatcher help us?' The eight-year-old was not joking – so prominent and powerful was 'Maggie' in the 1980s, the youngster obviously thought she could do anything.

> *It is God who judges: he brings one down, he exalts another.*
>
> Psalm 75:7

> *...there is no authority except that which God has established. The authorities that exist have been established by God.*
>
> Romans 13:1

It is better to take refuge in the LORD than to trust in man. It is better to take refuge in the LORD than to trust in princes.

Psalm 118:8-9

There are times when kings, presidents, emperors and prime ministers can seem all-powerful, but we must remember that their power comes from God. In a moment they can be deposed and in a relatively short time be forgotten. How much better to trust in the Eternal God than to have confidence in mortal man.

Sovereignty of God

(II)

All the sewage pipes were being renewed, and for our four-year-old son, the diggers, the wagons and the earth removers provided much excitement. Before work and after work, I had to take Andrew to see the men, the diggers and the deep holes.

The work went on for several weeks, and one evening, we were watching television downstairs when there was a deafening sound upstairs. Cautiously investigating the noise, I was shocked to discover that the plaster ceiling in our bedroom had come crashing down. If we had been in bed, the consequences could have been much more serious.

We were convinced, as were many others, that the foundation of the house had been disturbed by the roadworks, but our conviction was not shared by the insurance company. For Andrew, it all added to the excitement, but from then onwards, taking him to see the workmen did not have, for me, quite the same appeal.

> *When the foundations are being destroyed, what can the righteous do?*
>
> Psalm 11:3

The biblical foundations of creation, marriage, work, the Lord's Day are being eroded and destroyed, the effects of which are to be increasingly seen in our broken and secular society. 'What can the righteous do?' We can pray. We can maintain a consistent Christian testimony and we can continue to trust in a Sovereign God, whose ultimate purposes will never be destroyed.

> *For the earth will be filled with the knowledge of the glory of the LORD, as the waters cover the sea.*
>
> Habakkuk 2:14

SPIRITUAL RICHES

I was employed in banking from April 1967 until August 1970 – my original employer being Martins Bank, until they were taken over by Barclays Bank in December 1968. They were significant years, not just because they were my first introduction to the world of work but because it was during those years that I came to personal faith in Christ.

The bank's main branch was in Morecambe but there were sub branches at Bare and Heysham. These sub branches had reduced opening hours and the bank cashier was always accompanied by a guard. This was usually a retired man wanting to earn some extra money in order to supplement his pension.

These men differed in temperament, but my guard at Bare – Mr S – was a delight to work with. He was a raconteur, with a great sense of humour, and he kept me well supplied with cups of tea and coffee. One morning, he went to the bakery just opposite the bank and returned with some teacakes. He joined the queue at the till, and when he got to the counter, taking the teacake out of the bag, he said, 'John, can you please put this in my currant account?' Other customers had an air of disbelief – were their eyes and ears deceiving them? His humour might not have had the approval of the bank hierarchy, but it would have gone down well on Candid Camera.

...it was not with perishable things such as silver or gold that you were redeemed [...] but with the precious blood of Christ.

1 Peter 1:18-19

"Do not store up for yourselves treasures on earth where moth and rust destroy, and where thieves break in and steal. But store up for yourselves treasures in heaven, where moth and rust do not destroy, and where thieves do not break in and steal. For where your treasure is, there your heart will be also."

Matthew 6:19-21

However healthy or otherwise our bank accounts, we cannot buy or pay our way into heaven. But for those who trust in Christ, the deposit has already been paid and the investment already made. Through His death for sinners on the cross of Calvary, Jesus has opened their account in heaven.

Once opened, the believer can then invest in the 'Bank of Heaven'. This we do by alleviating the material needs of the poor, but principally by supporting the spread of the gospel. Are we storing up for ourselves treasures on earth or treasures in heaven?

SPIRITUAL VISION

For a number of years, my grandmother was almost blind, and this placed a strain upon her and also upon other members of the family. As a boy, I tried to help by reading to her the morning newspaper, but this was not without its difficulties. Grandma was very deaf, and hearing aids were not the sophisticated gadgets that they are today. Consequently, one had to 'shout' the news, but even then, Grandma could not always hear what was being said.

It was, therefore, a significant day when Grandma agreed to have a cataract operation. What today is a procedure accomplished in minutes was a far riskier operation in the 1950s and 1960s. The patient was in hospital for several days and after the operation had to lie immobile in a darkened room. When the bandages were eventually removed, they had to be replaced by thick glasses.

Grandma's sight was not in any way fully restored, but nevertheless, what a difference. She now had some sight and as well as walking unaided, she could, with the help of a magnifying glass, read newspapers and magazines by herself.

They came to Bethsaida, and some people brought a blind man and begged Jesus to touch him. He took the blind man by the hand and led him outside the village. When he had spat on the man's eyes and put his hands on him, Jesus asked, "Do you see anything?" He looked up and said, "I see people; they look like trees walking around." Once more Jesus put his hands on the man's eyes. Then his eyes were opened, his sight was restored, and he saw everything clearly.

Mark 8:22-25

Now we see but a poor reflection as in a mirror; then we shall see face to face. Now I know in part; then I shall know fully, even as I am fully known.

1 Corinthians 13:12

As believers our eyes have been opened but our 'spiritual vision' is not yet perfect. There are verses in the Bible we do not understand and providences we cannot make sense of. We 'see people [...] like trees walking' or we 'see a poor reflection as in a mirror'. Paul tells us, that is how it is 'now' but it is not how it shall be 'then'. In the words of Isaac Watts:

Then I shall see and hear and know
All I desired and wished below.
And every power find sweet employ
In that eternal world of joy.

TEMPTATION

Thursday was always 'baking day', and before school or during school holidays, my brother and I would 'help' our mother. The cake mixture was put in a bowl and with our individual spoons, it was our responsibility to stir the mixture. But on one occasion, as we stirred we also tasted, and as we continued to stir we also continued to taste. Not surprisingly, when mother came to see how we were doing, she was faced with two spoons, an empty bowl, but no cake mixture.

We did not force ourselves to eat what was before us and neither did we need any persuading. Not at all. It was attractive, tasty, tempting – to eat the mixture seemed the normal, the natural, thing to do.

> *When the woman saw that the fruit of the tree was good for food and pleasing to the eye, and also desirable for gaining wisdom, she took some and ate it. She also gave some to her husband, who was with her, and he ate it.*
>
> Genesis 3:6
>
> *...to enjoy the pleasures of sin for a short time.*
>
> Hebrews 11:25

There are times when sin is attractive and desirable; otherwise it would not be a temptation. However, temptation is only sin when we yield to Satan's evil suggestion. I suspect, having 'gorged' on the cake mixture, that later my brother and I had a sickly feeling. Pleasurable at first but then the consequences.

To Adam and Eve the temptation seemed irresistible, but the consequences for them and for us were horrendous. A fallen world, broken relationships – paradise turned into a 'vale of tears'. Let us remember this when the temptation appears so attractive and desirable. The pleasure comes before the pain.

THANKSGIVING

Mrs M. had been in hospital for surgery, and for a woman of her age was making a wonderful recovery. I visited her when she returned home, taking with me a 'get well' card. The room was full of cards and I commented how lovely it was to get so many greetings. My comment brought an unexpected response, as Mrs M., instead of being thankful for the cards she had received, began to castigate those who had not sent a card. They were most definitely 'named and shamed'.

> *Do everything without complaining or arguing.*
> Philippians 2:14

> *...give thanks in all circumstances; for this is God's will for you in Christ Jesus.*
> 1 Thessalonians 5:18

It is a sad trait of human nature, but we often find it easier to complain than we do to give thanks. The Apostle Paul tells us that to 'give thanks' is not just the polite thing to do; it is 'God's will'. As a believer, am I fulfilling the will of God by being a grateful person?

TIME (I)

In the 1960s, banks opened Monday to Friday from 10am to 3pm and on Saturdays from 9am to 12pm. Queues often formed, and so it was important that the doors were opened promptly on time. And this was one of the responsibilities of the office 'junior'.

Barry was a lovable but somewhat eccentric office 'junior', and one morning the doors had not been opened. 'Barry, it is ten o'clock,' said the chief cashier. 'Thank you, Mr Hughes,' said Barry and continued what he was doing. I had to gently explain to Barry that Mr Hughes was not so much telling him the time but asking for the bank doors to be opened.

> ...it is time to seek the LORD.
>
> Hosea 10:12

> ...now is the time of God's favour, now is the day of salvation.
>
> 2 Corinthians 6:2

What time is it? The Bible tells us, and yet many take no notice and continue with what they are doing. Nothing has really changed, for that was the response of the people in the days of Noah. They were told to take refuge in the Ark but the majority ignored Noah's pleading and tragically, when the flood came, they perished. Let us not ignore what time it is, and take action whilst we can.

TIME (II)

Mrs A. had reached the grand old age of one hundred, and a few days later, I called to see her. As I congratulated her on reaching this milestone, Mrs A. remarked, 'Oh, that's nothing – there is a woman a few doors away and she is two hundred.' 'Two hundred!' I said. 'Whatever do they feed you on around here?' When her granddaughter came into the room, I asked about this remarkable lady who was two hundred. It turned out she was in fact a hundred and two, but Mrs A. was still not altogether convinced.

> *What is your life? You are a mist that appears for a little while and then vanishes.*
>
> James 4:14

> *...do not forget this one thing, dear friends. With the Lord a day is like a thousand years, and a thousand years are like a day.*
>
> 2 Peter 3:8

> *Teach us to number our days aright, that we may gain a heart of wisdom.*
>
> Psalm 90:12

To us, one hundred years is a great age – and it is – and yet nothing compared to eternity. Methuselah lived to be 969, but again his time on earth was just a speck against the vastness of eternity. Time is short but its importance can never be underestimated, as our years on earth are preparation for eternity.

TIME (III)

When Andrew and Joanna were teenagers, on a Saturday, Pat and I tried to spend time with them. Andrew was a keen Morecambe Football Club supporter and Joanna was always happy in a shopping centre. Therefore, on this particular Saturday, I dropped Pat, Joanna and Aaron off in Pontefract town centre whilst Andrew and I proceeded to watch Morecambe at South Elmsall.

We had arranged to meet back in Pontefract at a quarter past five, but arriving at the agreed venue, there was no sign of Pat, Joanna and Aaron. It was in the days before mobile phones, and as the minutes ticked by, I wondered if Aaron had suffered an epileptic fit and been taken to hospital. We waited and waited until, at just after six o'clock, the 'wanderers' appeared.

They were quite relaxed and totally oblivious to the panic they had caused. Why? Well, Pat had gone into a shop and noticing the clock said half past three, she had adjusted her watch accordingly. However, Pat had not appreciated that this was the October night when the clocks were put back one hour and, in preparation for next week, the shop had already made this adjustment.

Consequently, Pat thought she was in time for our 17.15 rendezvous, when in fact it was almost 18.15. How she had managed to gain an hour without knowing was a mystery, but when we met up it was later – an hour later – than Pat had expected.

> *And do this, understanding the present time: the hour has already come for you to wake up from your slumber, because our salvation is nearer now than when we first believed. The night is nearly over; the day is almost here. So let us put aside the deeds of darkness and put on the armour of light.*
>
> Romans 13:11-12

Pat thought she knew the time but she didn't. Therefore, there was a lack of urgency, with Pat sauntering through the last hour, believing she had plenty of time. Paul says that, as believers, we do understand 'the present time'. We understand that with every passing day, we are one day nearer to heaven or to the return of Christ. And this should radically affect the kind of people that we are. The unbeliever does not know what time it is; he is not expecting either heaven or the return of Christ, and therefore, he sees no need to 'put aside the deeds of darkness'.

Clocks go back in October, but in the spiritual sense, no one can turn the clock back. The day we depart this world or the day Jesus comes again has already been fixed by God. Therefore, the believer should spend every day as though it were his last day – not sauntering or wasting his time, but each day seeking to be more like Christ and more active in His service. It is later than we think.

TONGUE

The hot summer of 2018 brought a huge moorland fire to an area of seven square miles above Bolton. The fire went on for forty-one days, and at its height there were over thirty-five engines, supported by specialist wildfire fighting teams from other areas of the country.

My four-year-old great-nephew could see the apocalypse from his home and was understandably concerned. Pausing for a moment, he then asked his mother if he could take a cup of cold water onto the moor and put the fire out.

Set a guard over my mouth, LORD; keep watch over the door of my lips.

Psalm 141:3

He who guards his mouth and his tongue keeps himself from calamity.

Proverbs 21:23

...the tongue is a small part of the body, but it makes great boasts. Consider what a great forest is set on fire by a small spark. The tongue also is a fire, a world of evil among the parts of the body.

James 3:5-6

Good for Jimmy that he wanted to put the fire out, but the blaze could never be extinguished with just a cup of water. In a similar way, the tongue can start a fire which sometimes, sadly, is never put out. How many unhappy, broken relationships begin when 'something is said' and it causes a hurt which is never healed.

The Bible has much to say about our mouths, our tongues, our lips, and it is wise counsel which we do well to follow. Once spoken, a word can never be returned and the damage caused can be irreparable.

TRIALS

Accompanied by Aaron in his wheelchair, we got on the train at Clitheroe and alighted at Bolton. To leave the station, one had either to use the lift or the stairs, but having the wheelchair, there was, for us, only one option. It was then that the problems started, as the lift was 'out of order'.

I went to an office on the station to be met by a most unhelpful man. His only suggestion was that we caught a train to Salford and then a train back from Salford to Bolton. We would then be on a platform where the lift was working. At first, I thought he was being humorous, but no, he was being deadly serious.

I declined his advice and went back to Pat and Aaron. We were pondering what to do when we were approached by a young man who, recognising our dilemma, asked if he could assist. To get off the platform, there were numerous steps to mount, but obtaining the help of two other men, we eventually managed to get the wheelchair up the stairs and out onto the streets of Bolton. How grateful we were to these men who put 'health and safety' considerations to one side and came to our rescue.

> *"If anyone would come after me, he must deny himself and take up his cross and follow Me."*
> Mark 8:34

"We must go through many hardships to enter the kingdom of God."

Acts 14:22

We do not want you to be uninformed about the hardships we suffered in the province of Asia. We were under great pressure, far beyond our ability to endure, so that we despaired even of life [...] you help us by your prayers.

2 Corinthians 1:8,11

It is rare for a person to be saved and then immediately be 'lifted' to heaven. We set out on a pilgrimage and we soon find there are 'stairs' to mount. 'Stairs' which are steep and 'stairs' which can cause us to feel tired and weary. We need helpers, those who will help us by prayer and support us when the way is uphill and strenuous. We need helpers – can we be a helper to others?

WITNESSING

Table tennis is a game I have played all my life. It began at school and continued throughout my days in the civil service. Since then, at family gatherings or Christian conferences, I have never been slow to pick up a bat and ball. I do not claim to be more than an average player, but it is a game which has brought me many hours of enjoyment.

The serve is one of the key skills a table tennis player can have, as the speed and spin of the ball can give the server an immediate advantage. Unfortunately, this is not a skill which I have ever altogether mastered. My strength is not in serving the ball but in being able to return it, and points are often won when opponents become frustrated as their 'smashes' are returned.

> *Let your conversation be always full of grace, seasoned with salt, so that you may know how to answer everyone.*
>
> Colossians 4:6

> *Always be prepared to give an answer to everyone who asks you to give the reason for the hope that you have.*
>
> 1 Peter 3:15

Few believers are called to preach, but every believer is required 'to give an answer'. When we are challenged about our Christian faith, we have to be able to 'get the ball back', to give reasons why we are Christians and why the faith we have embraced is relevant and logical.

Contact the Author

To contact the author, please write to:

John Mollitt,
5 Holme Park,
Burley-in-Wharfedale,
Bradford,
West Yorkshire,
LS29 7QT

Or send an email to:

john.mollitt@btinternet.com

Other Books by John Mollitt

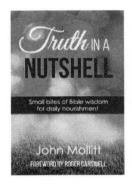

Truth in a Nutshell
ISBN 978-1-910197-76-9

This book of meditations contains over 100 scriptures and anecdotes. Taken from the life and experiences of itinerant preacher, John Mollitt, each story illustrates a key lesson from the scripture being studied.

How Shall They Hear?
ISBN 978-1-911086-43-7

This collection of memoirs paints the life of John Mollitt, a country preacher, in broad strokes, through poignant anecdotes that will at times make you smile, at other times pause to reflect.

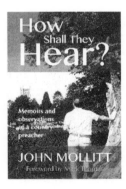

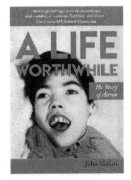

A Life Worthwhile
ISBN 978-1-78815-685-1

When a John and Pat Mollitt decide to adopt a severely handicapped boy, the lives of many are impacted by God's love and a child's smile.